Lunch Box
Letters

Joey Tripoli

ISBN 978-1-64559-519-9 (Paperback)
ISBN 978-1-64559-520-5 (Digital)

Covenant Books, Inc.
11661 Hwy 707
Murrells Inlet, SC 29576
www.covenantbooks.com

Unbecoming

How unbecoming I was,
as I was
unbecoming
who you made me to be.

I was unravelling
at every seam,
and being torn apart;
I was unbecoming
who I was…
betraying my own heart.

I let life
slowly etch away,
like a chisel to my frame,
all that made me who I was…
'til there was nothing left
but shame.

God forgive me
for unbecoming,
and unbecoming as I was…
thank you, Father,
for seeing beauty
'cause you looked at me
through love.

Acknowledgments

On the pages that follow, I will refer often to my dad, Joseph Tripoli, because it is in growing up as his daughter that I have felt the protective hand and the ardent heart of a father's love—that love that would do anything, give anything, for his child. And so thank you, Daddy, for showing me, in your human way, just how big our heavenly Father's heart is and how much he loves us![1]

Having acknowledged the depth of a father's love, which has inspired the writing of this book, I need to say that no one is more responsible for my relationship with God than my mom, Antonina Coppola. No one has spent more sleepless nights and tear-filled prayers on my behalf. Thank you, Mom.

---

[1] I struggled with choosing just the right word to describe a father's heart in that first sentence. "The _____ heart of a father's love…" I put so many different adjectives in that space over the years that it took me to write this book. Especially during the last few months, as I revised and edited over and over, I kept thinking, *What one word would capture the heart of not only a father, but of Our Father?* Different words, temporarily, held its place on this page—*compassionate, forgiving, loving*…But while all of them seemed to touch on one aspect of his heart, none of them said it all. Then one night as I was trying to sleep, but wrestling with this question, I finally just asked God, "God, what word would *you* choose to describe a father's heart, your heart?" Instantly, the word *ardent* came to my mind. I had no idea what that word meant, I had never heard it before. I rolled over and googled *ardent* on my phone. And this is what it said, "Enthusiastic or passionate. Synonyms: passionate, fervent, zealous, fervid, wholehearted, vehement, intense, fierce, fiery, burning, glowing, 'the ardent flames.'" *Whoa!* I thought, *Wow! That's what God's heart is like. That's how he loves us! His heart is burning for us like flames, intense, glowing.* I know this word came from God. Only he could have known the perfect word to describe his heart, his love, for us. It's a Father's love.

5

We, all of God's children, were created in his image and likeness. "So God created man in his own image, in the image and likeness of God, he created them; male and female he created them" (Genesis 1:27, AMP). We are made in his likeness—like him—that leads me to believe that God, in his personality, has both the protective nature of a father and the nurturing love of a mother. I am so grateful for both of my parents, here on earth, for reflecting to me a glimpse of our whole Creator and his awesome, fierce, love for us.

And last, but certainly not least, I am thankful for and to my son, Joshua, without whom I could never have understood how a parent's love for his or her child goes far beyond our ability to even comprehend and is, by our Creator's design, all-embracing! Knowing that the love I have for my son can never go away, no matter what, reminds me of what God's love is for us and that nothing can separate us from that love (Romans 8:37–39). Thank you, Joshua, for teaching me what unconditional and unending love really is.

Dear Daddy

The love between a doting father and his little girl is the closest thing I have to compare to God's love for us and what our relationship with him can be like. Again, only because I have been so blessed with a wonderful daddy-daughter relationship can I feel the similarities. The word *father*, or better yet *daddy*, speaks volumes to me. It speaks of a very special position and protective authority in my life.

I can recall, as a little girl, writing love letters to my dad. I would smile with anticipation as I hid each letter in between his sandwich bag and his industrial-sized-stainless-steel coffee thermos, and closed his giant lunch box. I couldn't wait for him to find it the next day. I knew he would light up when he discovered this little secret note just for him. I thought he might even brag to his friends (other construction workers on the job). "My little girl," he might say, "she's something special. She really loves me. Just look at all those XOXOXOXOs!"

As a grown-up now, I imagine a slightly different response— not so much a display of pride, but rather a tender smile, a heartfelt pause in his busy day of hard work. I can just see him quietly fold the letter back up and simply place it in the pocket of his worn-out, cement-covered flannel shirt, right there, close to his heart.

It's been years since I've helped pack my dad a lunch, but not so many that I can't remember the gist of what those little love letters would say. The always-cordial beginning, "Dear Daddy, Hi. How are you?" The simple body, "How is your day so far? If you're reading this, you're probably eating lunch. How is your lunch? I hope you're having a good day. I miss you. Hurry up and come home, but don't drive fast. Wear your seat belt. And don't smoke today." And of course, a most sincere closing, "I love you soooooooooo much! You're the best daddy in the whole wide world! XOXOXOXOXOXOXOXOXOXOXOXO" (until I ran out of space on the paper and the back of the paper). And then finally, "Love, Me." No need to formalize with a name; he knew who it was from. Oh, and throw in a bunch of hearts, smiley faces, flowers, and my best attempt at drawing a horse (his favorite animal), and there you have it—a beautiful love letter. I loved him so much, and I just wanted him to know it, to feel it, and to be proud.

I still have that old giant lunch box in my kitchen. It looks like a tackle box for fishing! My grandpa (my dad's dad) had the same kind, only metal, and that too sits proudly atop my kitchen cabinets—a fitting tribute to hard work and devotion to family.

Back to the intent of this book—how does this all relate? Well, the more grown-up I am, the more I have come to view my relationship with my heavenly Father as a precious daddy-daughter relationship.

Fearful of sounding disrespectful, I use the word *daddy* with great caution and reverence, and only to draw upon the connotations it holds. Our Father, in heaven, is the one and only true God. There is no other God but him. He is the King of kings and Lord of lords and the Creator of heaven and earth. He is our undefeatable Defender and Deliverer. He is our Rock and Redeemer. And still, he is our Father. Father... the title I'm most grateful he holds, the name I'm most thankful he bears. Father is the best name you'll ever get to call him because it implies closeness and connection. It acknowledges his authority and protective watch over you. You can cry out to him, as your Father, knowing full well that he loves you no matter how grown-up or worn-down you are, no matter how close you've stayed, or how far you've strayed. In your Father's eyes, you are still his precious little child, and in his eyes, the Son rises and shines on you, and makes you beautiful!

For some, this may seem like too much. You cannot relate to this kind of a father figure. You've never known any father like that. I understand; without an earthly frame of reference, this is hard to make sense of or even imagine. But take heart, your limited perspective or unfair experiences in no way limit your heavenly Father's ability and passion to love you. There is someone you can boldly and lovingly call, "Father," even if you never had a loving relationship with your father here on earth, and even if he was the last person you'd ever call on. This Father is different. This one is perfect, and he loves you perfectly.

In this book, I will bounce between prayers (I like to think of them as letters that I am writing to my heavenly Father), to poetry, to just getting my thoughts onto paper. I will write and pour out my heart to God, telling him how much I love him and long for him in my life. I will ask him questions and maybe in the process of writing and praying, hear his answers.

So if you want, join me on this journey—this journey that started off as journaling, but ended in a new revelation of God's love. This journey that took over eight years to put on paper, and will take a lifetime to walk. Cry with me in our shared pain, and smile with me in our shared relationship with our Father and in the realization of how much he loves us. And most importantly, praise him with me for all that he's done and will continue to do in our lives.

> To all who believed him and accepted him, he gave the right to become children of God. (John 1:12, NLT)

Dear Father,

Please guide this book and bless its readers. Share with me your wisdom and help me to know what say. I don't want to simply write down my own words—what good would they be to anyone? Rather, as I walk through this process of baring my soul and experiencing your love, let the words that you want heard flow through my pen and onto these pages. I'm just letting myself feel what I feel, exposing my heart, in faith, that you'll heal it, and in hopes that what I have to say may comfort even one person. So please, speak through me, write through me, and be with each person who is reading this. Chances are, if they're turning these pages, they have a heart that needs mending too. Be with them. In Jesus' name, I pray.

Love,
Me

The Sovereign Lord has given me his words of wisdom, so that I know how to comfort the weary. (Isaiah 50:4, NLT)

Butterfly

Like a delicate butterfly
on the side of the road,
her story unheard,
but not untold.

No sign of sorrow,
it's all inside,
but God knows it hurt...
God knows she cried.

Light as a feather
her wings held up high—
just her heart sank too heavy,
to let her fly.

Dear Father,

I wrote "Butterfly" years ago. You remember.
I was running, running away from another fight,
running from the pain. And there she was—this
delicate, dead butterfly just lying there, on the
side of the dirt road. I don't know how she died,
she looked completely untouched and intact.
Didn't matter though. She was dead. I picked
her up as gently as I could. *Why?* I thought. *Why
do I feel just like her?* Then I realized. No one
would have guessed, based on outward appear-
ances alone, how messed up she (or I) was on

the inside. There was no life left at all. So she lay there, discarded. It wouldn't be long until the earth remembered her no more. And that's just how I felt—and sometimes still feel. God, fix me. Breathe your life back into me.

Love,
Me

Treasures

Jesus said, "For where your treasure is, there your heart will be also" (Matthew 6:21, ESV). I know that to be true. The hard part, for me anyway, is that I've had to pick up and pack up my treasures so many times that I've lost my heart. I have lost, or had to let go of, so many of my treasures along the way. Those things and even people—which I held onto so dearly—are now gone. Treasures that, to me, defined my life and who I was are now faded memories. God, I'm so sorry I made them my treasure and in doing so put them above you. They held my heart captive. I should have known they'd never last. The only treasure worth holding onto is you. You free the heart! When my heart is held by, fixed on, or devoted to anything else but you, disappointment and bondage are sure to follow. And I'm left with an empty heart and full boxes.

Boxes

I've packed and unpacked
my treasures
so many times.
Each box holds the pieces
that fit together
to make up my broken life.

With every box I open,
memories float out
and fill my senses
with each detail of hope
I held at the time.

Now I just hold boxes,
and I try to keep them shut
so I can't see
or remember
the life
I thought I had.

I can't hold back my tears,
they flood out,
like the stories in each box,
and I try to reorganize
and give away my life
so it can't hurt me anymore.

I'm tired of emptying boxes,
but I can't pack them up
and go back
because the memories hurt,
but the life was killing me.

Father,

Forgive me for putting others and other things above you, for holding onto them tighter than I was holding onto you. I'm so sorry. And even though I feel like I'm losing so much of myself in this process, I know that it's only in letting go of the things of this world that I will become a light to shine in it. Only by "dying to myself" will I become fully alive and free in you. Help me, Father, to treasure you above all things and to let go of anything that holds me back from you, from anything that I cling to more than you. For nothing else can compare to you, and for you, I count it all loss.

Love,
Me

Indeed, I count everything as loss because of the surpassing worth of knowing Christ Jesus my Lord. For his sake I have suffered the loss of all things and count them as rubbish, in order that I may gain Christ and be found in him, not having a righteousness of my own that comes from the law, but which comes through faith in Christ, the righteousness from God that depends on faith. (Philippians 3:8–9)

The Heaviest Box

Everything's put away,
tidy and neat.
The boxes are stacked,
the packing's complete.
The smell of cardboard fills the air
like depressing potpourri,
reminding you,
"Life's not fair,"
not how it's "posta" be.
The bags are full,
each sealed and tied,
secure with a double knot.
Once again,
"Life's not fair,"
(just in case you forgot).
With my own two hands
and my own weak arms,
I lift and carry it all away.
Down the stairs,
to the truck…
nothing here can stay.
Just one more box.
There it is.
And no matter how I try,
I just can't seem to lift this one,
I just can't say, "Goodbye."
It's the heaviest box.
It's just so heavy,

in my arms and in my mind.
I can't carry it with me,
but I can't leave it behind.
I can't lift it, God.
I can't put it away.
And more and more
of myself
goes in it
every
day.

Good Gifts

Dear God,

Why is this so hard? It feels like it should get easier, but it doesn't. Sadness just sits here like an unwelcome guest who's made my heart its home. I've tried being polite and asking it to leave. I've gotten fed up and tried kicking it out, but it hasn't left. I'm beginning to understand that sadness is one of the most stubborn guests we can entertain, it just lingers. Its presence is heavy and continuous. It's not going to leave on its own, and I can't get rid of it by myself, so I need you, Lord, to escort it to the door. Make it go away. Kick it to the curb and lock the doors of my heart behind it. I need you, Father. I can't do this on my own.

Love,
Me

Make It Go Away

God, do you see me?
Do you see me down here?
Is this what I asked for?
Did I bring this upon myself?
What do you want from me?
Is this from you?

It doesn't feel like a Father's gift...
Yet, I stood there with empty hands.
Which is worse?
Will this ever get better?
Is this what I've done?
Or what you've done?
Whatever it is,
Whoever it's from,
Make it end.
Please...
Make it go away.

As a little girl, my daddy was my hero (still is). I believed he was my "knight in shining armor," who could, and would, banish whatever or whoever threatened me. Thank God, many dads, as imperfect as they may be, know how to protect their children and shower them with love and, yes, gifts. God's Word says, "So if you sinful people know how to give good gifts to your children, how much more will your heavenly Father give good gifts to those who ask him" (Matthew 7:11, NLT).

I would conclude then, if our earthly fathers love us so much, that they want and know how to give us good gifts, they would also love us so much that they would want and know how to protect us from any danger, to spare us from any heartache, if they could. Here lies the unhappy ending to our fairy tale—they can't.

They can't protect us from harm, rejection, grief, or loss. They can't protect our bodies, our hearts, or our minds. They can't shield us from death or even life.

What about our heavenly Father? He's bigger! He's stronger! He's more powerful; in fact, he's all-powerful! Why doesn't he shield us from pain? Why doesn't he just make it go away? I know he *could*, but he doesn't, not always. So I have to believe that in "it" (the pain, humiliation, loss, whatever "it" is) lies the gift—a good gift that only a loving Father would give. Oh, our happy ending may just come after all!

We don't always get the gift we ask for, and even if we do, we may not get it in the way we thought we would. Sometimes our Father, in his wisdom, wants to teach us something in the process. "'For my thoughts are not your thoughts, neither are your ways my ways,' declares the Lord" (Isaiah 55:8, NIV). Let me illustrate this point with a story.

When I was eleven years old, I was out Christmas shopping with my mom and dad. I saw a display in the window of a Hallmark store; it was a giant Rodney Reindeer stuffed animal, holding a sign that he could be won. He sat there among all the Christmas decorations that filled the showcase. He was huge, bigger than me, and I fell in love with him immediately. His big eyes stared back at me through the window like he was telling me he needed a home, and I decided his home was going to be with me. I went into the store to see him up close and learned that they were having a raffle. I could put my name in the drawing and win him! I was so excited and quickly entered my name.

To buy Rodney, it would have cost $150, and I knew there was no chance of getting him that way. I spent too many years wearing hand-me-downs and buying "new" school clothes at the Salvation Army to think for a second that we could afford him, but that was okay. I was going to win him. I prayed to God to please let my name be picked. I asked my mom and dad to pray too, and I was sure that God would answer this prayer. For some reason, I had complete faith that I was going to get him. It wasn't just wishful thinking—I was sure. My parents kept trying to prepare me "just in case" I didn't win. They didn't want my faith to be shattered. I wasn't worried though, I had no doubt in my mind.

Well, the contest came and went, and I never heard from the store. I was shocked and very disappointed, even embarrassed, because I had proclaimed to everyone that I was going to win Rodney. I had drawn pictures of him everywhere and had a special place already prepared for him in my room.

But they never called. I didn't win. I couldn't believe it. He wasn't mine. I didn't understand because I had read in the Bible many verses about asking for what you want in Jesus' name (which I did) and if you didn't doubt (which I didn't), then you would receive what you asked for (but I didn't). I had done everything I learned and believed I should—and it didn't work.

But on Christmas morning when I walked down the hallway and into the living room, I saw Rodney sitting there, right in front of our fireplace, holding my Christmas stocking! I was completely overwhelmed with surprise and gratitude! *How did he get there? I didn't win...*

The only smile bigger than mine, that morning, was my dad's. He later told me that he had a feeling I might not win, and he was worried that I'd be crushed since my faith had been so strong. I was so thankful, and I still am. I still have that stuffed animal, and every time I see it, it reminds me of a very important lesson.

The lesson God taught me years later, through this, was that if I would have received this gift the way I thought best, by winning it in the contest, then that's all I would have received—the gift. But the way God did it, I received much more than just the gift; I learned something about the giver of the gift, and how much he loves me. I learned about a father's love. In answering my prayer this way, God taught me that a father knows how to give good gifts and is willing to sacrifice for his children.

I know that $150 back then was a crazy amount of money to spend on a stuffed animal. (It still is!) My dad worked very hard for his money, and there wasn't a lot of extra. I know the sacrifice he made to be able to give me a good gift that Christmas. What he didn't know, and what I didn't realize until years later, was that the real gift was learning about his love for me. And that gift is priceless.

> So if you sinful people know how to give good gifts to your children, how much more will your heavenly Father give good gifts to those who ask him. (Matthew 7:11, NLT)

You can trust God. Sometimes the gift isn't what you expected. Sometimes it's wrapped in confusion, disappointment, or even pain.

But trust him. There may be a lesson inside that is far is more valuable than what you asked for.

> "My thoughts are nothing like your thoughts,"
> says the Lord. "And my ways are far beyond any-
> thing you could imagine." (Isaiah 55:8, NLT)

Beautiful

As age and years of hard work began to wear on my dad's body, he would spend the coldest months down south where the warm weather was kinder to his sore bones and tired muscles. I remember one year, after a long winter of not seeing him and missing him so much, he finally came home. As soon as he got back, I made plans to see him. We met that morning for breakfast (something we did very often).

I love meeting my dad for breakfast. I just have to laugh, though, because he always tells me I'm beautiful. Like I said, I have to laugh. I guess that's what they mean by "beauty is in the eye of the beholder." *Beautiful* is hardly the word I would choose, especially since I have to meet him at the crack of dawn because that's what his routine dictates. I look and feel like I just crawled out of bed (because I did). But he thinks I'm beautiful.

As soon as he sees me, his face lights up like the sunrise (which just happens to be the name of the restaurant where we always meet, the Sunrise Family Diner). Now I feel "beautiful," or should I say, I feel "loved." It's his love that makes me feel that way. His eyes well up with love, and his face beams with pride, and he tells me how beautiful I am. How beautiful I *am*, not how beautiful I *look*. *Am* is a verb of being, not doing. And you see, I don't have to *do* anything to be beautiful to my dad.

You know what's even better than that? Our heavenly Father feels the exact same way about us! That's right; every time he looks at you, he sees your beauty. It doesn't matter how you feel or how you look, you just *are*—beautiful.

When I'm at breakfast with my dad, not only does he make sure everyone sees me with him, but he is certain that everyone sees me the way he does. He jokes around with all his buddies, and I blush with embarrassment, as I think, *Come on Dad, you're the only one here who sees me that way.*

And that may very well be true. He could be, and probably is, the only one in that restaurant (or in the whole world for that matter) who thinks I'm beautiful, and you know what? That's enough for me! Because when you're in your father's presence, and you feel his love, and understand the way *he* sees you, it's enough to believe it. You know you are loved beyond measure. It's that all-embracing love—nothing can compare to it or stand against it. It's how we love our children. It's how God loves us.

What someone else may think or say about you fades away and cannot hold up against what your Father says. And your Father in heaven says, "You're beautiful."

Now, I don't know if you had the blessing of feeling your earthly dad's love like that. I can only hope you have, but I know many dads down here don't get it. They're broken themselves, wounded by their own lives. We all are. And maybe your dad was messed up, and hurtful toward those he should have shown love. Many dads don't know how to let themselves feel love, let alone show it. However, I don't have to hope that your heavenly Father loves and delights in you and knows how to show it.

> The Lord delights in you and will claim you as
> His own. (Isaiah 62:4, TLB)

> But God demonstrates his own love for us in
> this: While we were still sinners, Christ died us.
> (Romans 5:8, NIV)

So what do you do if you feel like your dad down here didn't delight in you? What if you grew up in a house where *loved* and *beautiful* were the last things you ever felt? Choose to listen to what God, your Father in heaven, says about you, knowing he never lies and he is never wrong. You see, the message you've heard from your dad (or anyone else) that was deliberately, or even unintentionally, void of love does not have to speak louder or longer than God's message of love to you. It shouldn't, and it can't because God's words are truth, and the truth will set your heart free—free from believing the wrong messages any longer. You are God's masterpiece (Ephesians 2:10)! He created you, and he knows you better and sees you more clearly than anyone else. Spend time in his love. Give your insecurities to him, and he will heal them. Get in his presence, and he will shine upon you like the sunrise, and you will feel loved and beautiful like you are.

The more time you spend with your heavenly Father, the more you will realize that there's nothing better. You will never feel more love than when you're surrounded by his unconditional and overwhelming love for you. You will never feel more peace than when you lay it all at his feet—all your worries, fears, and insecurities. You will never feel more joy than when you let him be your strength and start getting excited about all he can and will do in your life. You will never feel more hope than when you realize all things are possible with him. You see, it just doesn't get any better than being in your Father's presence.

> Better is one day in your courts than a thousand elsewhere. (Psalm 84:10, NIV)

I understand this may all be new for you, especially if you grew up without ever feeling this kind of love, peace, joy, or hope. But even if no one has been able to give this to you before, praise our heavenly Father that "God can do what men can't" (Luke 18:27, TLB). Maybe your dad couldn't, or wouldn't, give you the love you were born to receive. Maybe he didn't instill in you the assurance you needed, or confidence in who you are—God's uniquely beautiful creation—but your Father can and will. All you have to do is listen to him, and then believe what he tells you. You can believe him.

> Those who look to him are radiant; their faces are never covered with shame. (Psalm 34:5, NIV)

Humpty Dumpty

No one (not even the best dad in the world) can ever heal our broken, beaten hearts. But God can. In Isaiah 61, we read that God sent his Son to bind up our wounds and comfort our broken hearts. It's kind of silly, but for some reason, this makes me think of that old nursery rhyme, "Humpty Dumpty." I was playing around with its words and came up with the following:

> My hopeful heart sat on a wall,
> My hopeful heart had a great fall,
> All the king's horses,
> And all the king's men
> Could not put my heart
> Back together again.

You see, none of the king's horses, none of the king's men—no one—but the King himself (the King of kings and Lord of lords) can put your heart back together again. Only he can heal your heart after it breaks. And if you're like me, not only has your heart been broken, it's been crushed and ground to ashes. But even then, he can put it back together again. Thank God for his Son, Jesus, who came to us to give us "beauty for ashes; joy instead of mourning; praise instead of heaviness" (Isaiah 61:3, TLB). Thank God for him because there's no one else who is able.

As much as your dad may have loved to have been able to fix your broken heart, he couldn't, and he can't. As much as they want to, your parents, spouse, friends, counselor, pastor, children (whoever you *think* is responsible for and capable of comforting you), cannot heal your heart. Even if they try, they will fail miserably. That is not what they were sent to do. You are looking to the wrong source. Only Jesus was sent "to comfort the brokenhearted" (Isaiah 61:1, TLB).

Your friends and family didn't knit your heart together in the first place—your heavenly Father did. "For you created my inmost being; you knit me together in my mother's womb" (Psalm 139:13, NIV). No one, not even your mother, in whose womb you were "knit together," formed your heart and knows it like God does. No one else can truly understand your heart. It's unique to you, and the only one who knows it, understands it, and can heal it is the One who created it in the first place.

Dear Father,

Thank you for staying so close to me while my heart is breaking. Thank you for not leaving me alone in my misery, alone in this storm. Only you know how my heart works and how it got this way. Only you understand. Only you feel my pain along with me. Help me to remember not to go running to others for comfort. Keep me from constantly going to others for answers. Oh, when will I learn that no one can provide for me but you? When I look to others, not only are they destined to disappoint me (because they're not you), but even their best attempts muddle the one voice I should be listening to—yours. I'm so sorry for having done this so many times. I need only you. I need you desperately. Thank you that I can trust you with my whole, be it broken, heart.

Love,
Me

The Lord is close to the brokenhearted; he rescues those whose spirits are crushed. (Psalm 34:18, NLT)

I will not leave you comfortless: I will come to you. (John 14:18, KJV)

No, I will not abandon you or leave you as orphans in the storm—I will come to you. (John 14:18, TLB)

Hand to Hold

When I'm alone
No one's hand to hold
When I'm feeling forgotten,
Misused and old…
That's when my Father
Reminds me
Of whose hands I'm in
And how He's lifted me up
Out of heartache and sin.

He tells me,
You're my daughter,
You're in the palm of my hand.
You *feel* lonely,
But you are not alone.
You *feel* sad,
But I am healing your heart.
You just can't see it
Because it's so much bigger
Than your vision.
So close your eyes.
Lean back.
Feel my hand around you,
On all sides.

You're looking for a hand to hold;
But I'm telling you,
Look to the hand that holds you.

I will never drop you,
I will never let you go.
You will never have to search
For another hand to hold you.
Look no further
I've got you.

Love,
Your Father

The Rescue

I'm beginning to realize, more and more, that God, our Father, is roaring mad when someone deliberately causes us pain. Yes, he is merciful and forgiving, full of loving kindness, slow to anger; but when someone willfully and purposefully chooses to hurt you, his child, he's not the distant faraway-on-his-throne God (who too many of his children imagine and settle for), he's your *Father*.

He's not going to let someone get away with hurting you whether you see his vengeance and justice played out or not—it will be done. His wrath burns as fervently as his love! Remember his heart is "ardent," as fierce and consuming as flames! Again, I wish everyone had a physical fatherly example to link to this, but even if you don't, that's okay. You have the biggest, strongest Father—not only *in the whole wide world*, but the Creator of *the whole wide world*—holding you in his hands, not because you climbed up high enough to crawl in there, but because he scooped down low enough to pick you up. No matter how old you are or how far you've drifted or fallen, you are his precious child, and he loves you with a Father's love.

> Even to your old age and gray hairs I am he, I am
> he who will sustain you. I have made you and I
> will carry you; I will sustain you and I will rescue
> you. (Isaiah 46:4, NIV)

It is your Father's will to rescue you, protect you, and hold you. If you'll let him, he'll hold you forever. It's never him who lets go. He will carry you, sustain you, and never forget you.

> Behold, I have engraved you on the palms of
> my hands; your walls are continually before me.
> (Isaiah 49:16, ESV)

What walls have you built around yourself? Around your heart? How have you attempted to protect yourself rather than allow or trust your Father to do so? He will hold you, he will fight for you, and he will protect you. Just like a father, he explains to us that when we're hurt, he's hurt. If you're a parent, you understand this. If someone hurts your baby, they're hurting you, and there's nothing that hurts worse. So when someone does us harm, it's as if they're doing it to him. That's how close he is; that's how connected we can be to him.

> The Lord of Glory has sent me against the nations
> that oppressed you, for he who harms you sticks
> a finger in Jehovah's eye. (Zechariah 2:8, TLB)

And yet, as Christians, we may think that we're supposed to suffer, even that God wants us to suffer. For some reason, we believe that not only is he *not* terribly angry when we suffer at the hands of others, but that he's actually somehow glorified. Now I'm not a theologian or a scholar, but I think that the glory he gets is not when we suffer, but when we *overcome* the suffering. Yes, he will use our pain and suffering for our good and for his glory because he doesn't waste anything, but it's in the victory that his glory is revealed. So along those lines, suffering is necessary but not necessarily glorious. When we triumph, however, and rise above our suffering, and we thank and praise him even in our suffering, *then* he is glorified. That's glorious!

His face doesn't light up with pride when we're lying in a pool of our own tears. He's not grinning from ear to ear when we're suffering at the hands of others. When we're in anguish, he's not rejoicing. His heart's not bursting when ours are being crushed. And I hardly think he would call us his "pride and joy," when we're wallowing around in self-pity.

> But you have not praised the God who gives you the breath of life and controls your destiny. (Daniel 5:23, TLB)

Praise—that's how we overcome suffering. That's how we bring glory to our Father! So then does suffering lead to glory? Yes! Paul says it in Romans 8:17 (TLB), "And since we are his children, we will share his treasures—for all God gives to his Son Jesus is now ours too. But if we are to share his glory, we must also share his suffering." It gets better; remember that happy ending I alluded to earlier? Here it is. The gift that our loving Father longs to give us is the glory that follows, "Yet what we suffer now is nothing compared to the glory he will reveal to us later" (Romans 8:18, NLT).

We suffer. It's a way of life down here. Jesus himself had to suffer. He suffered greatly, far more than any of us ever will, and was killed, in our place. That was the sacrifice, the suffering, the death, and the burial. But the glory was when he rose again! He overcame— that's how God was glorified.

Do you think our Father looked away as Jesus hung there on the cross because he felt glorified in his Son's suffering? His only begotten Son, with whom he was well-pleased, was nailed to a cross to die a shameful and agonizing death. I don't think he felt glory. I think he felt pain, the bitterest anguish possible. I think God Almighty was sad beyond even his own belief; he *had* to look away.

The glory wasn't felt in his child's suffering. But how do you think he felt when his Son rose again above all that suffering, defeating death and defying the grave, overcoming Satan and all sin, and accomplishing the purpose for which he was sent? That's when, I'm sure, he beamed with Fatherly pride. "That's my Son!" he must have exclaimed to all of heaven and earth. When Jesus Christ rose victorious, his Father (our Father) was glorified. And each time we rise victorious, by God's grace, we too bring him glory, and all of heaven rejoices!

I truly believe God wants us to know that he loves us just as much as he loves Jesus. He is a righteous, perfect Father—he has no favorites. Therefore, we can be assured that he groans with us in our suffering and rejoices with us in our victories just like he did with Jesus, just like we do with our own children.

God doesn't relish in our trials and tribulations or even in teaching us a lesson. He disciplines us, not for pleasure but for our own good. "For the Lord disciplines those he loves, and he punishes each one he accepts as his child" (Hebrews 12:6, NLT). If you're a parent, you can relate to this. Disciplining your child is not fun. You don't enjoy it. It may even hurt you more than it does your child, but you do it out of love and protection. Again, we were made in God's image, and here, it's easy to see where we get our parenting style. We're like this with our kids because we're like him, and that's how he is with us, his children.

> "Is not Israel still my son, my darling child?" says the Lord. "I often have to punish him, but I still love him. That's why I long for him and surely will have mercy on him." (Jeremiah 31:20, NLT)

As a mom, I can most certainly relate. When I have to discipline my son, I do so because I have a moral obligation to teach him right from wrong. I'm not seeking to control his life or wreck his fun. I just want to protect him from harm. I have a responsibility to nurture and guide him along the right path. When he strays off that path, wanders into darkness, and gets lost, I desperately search and pray for him. I do everything in my power to help him come back. My heart aches until he returns and when he does, I am overjoyed! When he learns and overcomes, we can celebrate the victory together. We grow in closeness through these life lessons. Our relationship with our Father is no different. My son doesn't have to earn my love back or fear condemnation when asking for forgiveness, and neither do we. "Oh, return to me, for I have paid the price to set you free," is what we can hear our Father saying to us (Isaiah 44:22b, NLT).

So if you're going through a difficult time, if you feel stuck in the suffering or feel like you're being disciplined, turn to your Father, the only one who knows exactly what you're going through, who knows the most intimate details of your pain. Whether your pain was brought on by others or all by yourself, God doesn't want you to stay beneath it. He wants to lift you up and over it. Discipline, as deserved as it may be, is not your Father's ultimate desire for you just like it's not our ultimate desire for our children. God wants you to come back to him and all he has for you. He wants restoration. It's the same thing we want with our kids when they wander off, right? We want them to turn around and come back home! And so does he.

Turn around, run back to your Father, and ask him to help you. He will. Choose to learn from your pain and get back up. Choose to overcome. Choose to forgive and let go of whatever it is that keeps you suffering. Choose to turn away from it and set your gaze on him. He longs to free you from that bondage. Don't stay in your pain. That's not what he wants for you. He tells you what he wants.

> I want your promises fulfilled. I want you to trust
> me in your times of trouble, so I can rescue you,
> and you can give me glory. (Psalm 50:15, TLB)

See, like any good father would, God wants to rescue you. And when you let him, when you let him lift you up and out of your suffering, that's when he's glorified. "When we were utterly helpless with no way of escape, Christ came at just the right time" (Romans 5:6, NLT). The glory is in the rescue—at just the right time, the overcoming, the victory!

> The righteous person faces many troubles, but
> the Lord comes to the rescue each time. (Psalm
> 34:19, NLT)

The Lord says, "I will rescue those who love me. I will protect those who trust in my name. When they call on me, I will answer; I will be with them in trouble. I will rescue them and honor them. I will reward them with a long life and give them my salvation." (Psalm 91:14–16, NLT)

Shake the Dust from Your Feet

Whatever happens to the princess once she's rescued? We never learn this in fairy tales because that's where the story always ends. But that's not where our story ends when the Prince of Peace rescues us. When we reach up and grab ahold of his hand, he pulls us out of whatever pit we've sunk into, and a whole new story begins, if we let it. "He lifted me out of the pit of despair, out of the mud and mire. He set my feet on solid ground and steadied me as I walked along" (Psalm 40:2, NLT). Now we must learn *how* to walk along more closely with God so we don't fall into another pit, or the same one for that matter, and so we can begin to enter into all he has for us.

Sometimes that's hard. However, when I'm in trouble, I know I can call on my heavenly Father for help. He may not swoop down and rescue me right away. I may need to right some wrongs I've done or learn my way through and overcome. In the end though, once I have overcome or been freed from a trial, I owe all the glory to God who held me in his hand the whole time and made me victorious through his grace. And then I must learn to walk more closely with him. So even once I'm *out* of trouble, that doesn't mean I'm trouble-free. There will still always be challenges.

> In this world you will have trouble. But take heart! I have overcome the world. (John 16:33, NIV)

Once I'm out of my pit of despair and on solid ground, sometimes I don't know what to do next. I know I am supposed to walk more closely with God, but I'm not sure how to take the first few steps. I second-guess myself and my ability to stay on solid ground.

I may even start to doubt or wonder if I really am on solid ground. Did God really *deliver* me? I know I don't deserve that kind of unfailing love, so I question it. How could I be entitled to such grace? I certainly haven't always shown it to others. I start doubting my right to be free.

It's the enemy. The accuser. It's as if he's standing right there on my shoulder, whispering in my ear, "Did God really *rescue* you? You're just trying to make yourself feel better, but you can't get out of this. This is the life you've made."

I was feeling this way one morning. As soon as I opened my eyes to start a new day, the accuser was right there. Guilt. *Ugh! How could I have messed up so badly? How could I have been so wrong? Why am I so—?* But God stopped me, then and there. (You see, he was right there too.) He said, "Shake the dust from your feet." I pondered those words. *What?* Then I started to doubt they were from God. *Can I really hear him? Am I just making this stuff up? No, I'm not! Why would those words just pop in my head? Those aren't my words! I don't talk like that!* And the more I trusted that—yes, God does actually talk to me (and to anyone who will listen)—the more I could understand what he was telling me.

Over two thousand years ago, Jesus had actually told his disciples the same thing. He told them, when they go into a town to preach his name but are not received there, they are to leave and shake the dust from their feet. "If any household or town refuses to welcome you or listen to your message, shake its dust from your feet as you leave" (Matthew 10:14, NLT). The same instructions are recorded in Mark 6:11 and Luke 9:5, as well. So these aren't *my* words. I wasn't making it up.

As to the meaning and why it pertained to me that morning, I believe God was telling me to move on. Yes, I have made some wrong choices, believed some lies, and made some mistakes; but that doesn't mean I need to remain in guilt for the rest of my life. That doesn't mean I need to stay wrapped in those chains. I could stop wondering why things happened the way they did and just move on. I could stop doubting my instincts and my own feelings. I could stop drowning in my remorse. I could move on from my regrets, shake its dust from my feet, and just keep walking—walking more closely with God.

So here it is, my attempt to brush off the dirt from my fall, to clean myself up, and wipe the tears off my muddy face. This is me, shaking the dust from my feet and moving on.

Shake the Dust from Your Feet

When I am not received
And can't compete,
What do I do, Lord?
"Shake the dust from your feet."

When no one picks me up,
Though I'm tired and beat,
How can I rise, Lord?
"Shake the dust from your feet."

When they all drink to life
Of barley and wheat,
But I'm drained and I'm parched…
"Shake the dust from your feet."

When I try to be loved,
To belong, and be sweet,
But I'm laughed at and mocked…
"Shake the dust from your feet."

When I walk down a road
With no "middle to meet,"
How far do I go, Lord?
"Shake the dust from your feet."

When my heart's been trampled
'Neath steel-toe and cleat,

Do I toughen and take it?
"Shake the dust from your feet."

When truth's cleverly told
In a world of deceit,
Do I live in the dark?
"Shake the dust from your feet."

When I'm stripped of my pride
While they're clothed in conceit,
Do I turn back and grovel?
"Shake the dust from your feet."

Dear Father,

Thank you for these words. Even now as I reread them and relive them, they help me to tune out the accusing voice of the enemy. Oh, Prince of Peace, rescue me, daily if need be, from my own condemning thoughts and quiet me with your love.

Love,
Me

And his name will be called Wonderful Counselor, Mighty God, Eternal Father, Prince of Peace. (Isaiah 9:6, ESV)

Peace I leave with you; my peace I give to you. Not as the world gives do I give to you. Let not your hearts be troubled, neither let them be afraid. (John 14:27, ESV)

Even if we feel guilty, God is greater than our feelings, and he knows everything. (1 John 3:20, NLT)

You gave me victory over my accusers. (Isaiah 52:2, ESV)

Shake yourself from the dust and arise; be seated, O Jerusalem; loose the bonds from your neck, O captive daughter of Zion. (Isaiah 52:2, ESV)

One God

There is one Lord, one faith, one baptism, and one God and Father, who is over all and in all and living through all.

—Ephesians 4:5–6 (NLT)

Dear Father,

It comforts me, and I hope it comforts others, that you are *over all.* You are above everything and everyone. You are the absolute authority and final say *in all* things. Thank you for being so big!

You are working *through all* the things that I go through. Every situation in which I find myself, every emotion I feel, every problem I encounter, every challenge I face, every dream I dream, every plan I make, *everything* must bow its knee to you. As do I.

Thank you. I don't want to be the one in control, not even of my own life. I'll mess it up. But you—alive and working in me and through me—now that's a different story! With you, all things are possible (Matthew 19:26), so I want you in control of my everything! I bow my every thought, hope, and dream before you. I submit all things to you, Father. You're in charge. And I thank you for it!

You are Lord over all! That means you can release or halt whatever you choose. God, why don't your people fear you more, myself included? When I consider your power and might, your supremacy, I should be in constant reverent awe of you and your holiness! I want this realization ever before me because when I am aware (or reminded) of just who you are, I need fear nothing else! Your Word says, "If God is for us, who can ever be against us?" (Romans 8:31, NLT).

That's right, when I am reminded of who you are, then I am reminded of who I am in you. I am your daughter! Anyone who tries to get to me is going to have to go through you! I'm not scared anymore.

Love,
Me

"As surely as I live," says the Lord, "every knee will bend to me, and every tongue will confess and give praise to God!" (Romans 14:11, NLT)

The Lord of Heaven's Armies has spoken—who can change his plans? When his hand is raised, who can stop him? (Isaiah 14:27, NLT)

Yes, and from ancient of days I am he. No one can deliver out of my hand. When I act, who can reverse it? (Isaiah 43:13, NIV)

Dear Father,

Since you are over all things, you have the power to start and finish whatever you want. Thank you that when you say, "Enough," that's it. Enough is enough when you say it. Others may say it, even myself, and not mean it. But your word is final.

You said, "Enough!" I remember, I heard you. I was living a life of constant defeat, banging my head against the wall. I know much of it was my own fault, much of it also the pain and bitterness brought on by a broken heart. It didn't matter—it was still "enough."

I love you, Father, and I am so thankful that when you feel my heartache and see my downward spiral, there comes a point when even you can't take it anymore, and you say, "Enough!"

You can start things and you can stop them—makes sense; after all, you are "the Alpha and the Omega, the First and the Last, the Beginning and the End" (Revelations 22:13, NLT). When the Alpha and the Omega says, "Enough," you better believe it's over. When the Beginning and the End says, "The End," close the book.

Enough

You saw me cry
You saw me die
A thousand deaths
Of hopeless breaths

You saw me strive
You saw me bend
You saw me snap
And reach my end

You saw me wilt
Beneath my pain
You saw me hang
My head in shame

You lifted me
Above the rain
You shined your Light
And called my name

You carried me
You even cried
You said, "Enough!
For you…
I died."

I just want to mention here, "Close the book," was something that my dad and his dad (Grandpa Tripoli) used to always say when the discussion was over. If we were talking about something and it got to the point where they felt that the discussion needed to be done, that is how they would end it. When they decided that it was enough, they would simply take their hands and gesture closing a book and say, "Close the book." And that was it. Conversation over.

Dear Father,

Thank you for knowing when to "close the book." Thank you that you know my breaking point better than I do, and for being ready to step in and save me at just the right time. Thank you for sending your Son to redeem my broken life. Thank you for knowing when enough was enough and once again, rescuing me.

Love,
Me

Keep me as the apple of your eye; hide me in the shadow of your wings. (Psalm 17:8, NIV)

"On that day I will gather you together and bring you home again. I will give you a good name, a name of distinction, among all the nations of the earth, as I restore your fortunes before their very eyes. I, the Lord, have spoken!" (Zephaniah 3:20, NLT)

Daddy, Drive Me Home

This isn't just
A fork in the road,
It's a knife in my heart,
Sharp and cold.

I can't find the words,
Nothing makes sense.
The night swirls around me,
Paved in pretense.

I need You to help me,
I can't do it on my own
Your answer awaits me,
Your will, still, unknown.

Black ice and glare...
Can't see where I'm going,
Spinning out of control,
Am I reaping or sowing?

I'm not gonna make it
Out here on my own,
I need you to get me,
Daddy, drive me home.

I remember being somewhere at night when I was younger and just knowing I needed to leave. I remember being old enough to drive myself but still calling my dad to come get me. I felt safer when I knew he was behind the wheel, and I knew that I could always call him, no matter where I was or how late it had gotten, and he'd jump in his truck and come get me and drive me home. How much more is our heavenly Father always available to us, always waiting for us to cry out to him, "Daddy, drive me home!"

Have you ever gotten yourself in a situation in which you saw no way out—not on your own anyway? Have you driven yourself so far away and taken so many wrong turns that now you don't know how to get back home, or even back to "you?" Call your Father—he's up. He's waiting for you. And he's willing, even wanting, to come get you. He's not going to reprimand or belittle you with questions and accusations. He's going to thank you for calling him. He's going to get in the driver's seat, if you'll let him, and take you back. Why would he do this? Because you're his child, and he loves you.

Dear Father,

Thank you for always "taking my call" no matter how late it is or how much trouble I've gotten myself into. Thank you for answering whenever I cry out to you. It doesn't matter what I've done or how lost I've gotten—you're still just one call away. Thank you for being such a faithful, loyal Father. I know I never have to stay lost. You tell me in your Word that I will find you when I look for you with all my heart. And I do. With all my heart, Lord, I seek you.

Thank you for never leaving me lost and in darkness. You've always been there, you've never left my side. You truly are the Good Shepherd. And a good shepherd never leaves his sheep. Through all the storms, you are here. Help me to remember to look only to you and to cling to you alone. That way, I can say, "I do follow the Good Shepherd, and I do know his voice, and the voice of a stranger I will not follow" (John 10:4–5).

You're as close to me as my next breath. Where could I go from your presence? Nowhere! King David understood this truth: "I can never escape from your Spirit! I can never get away from your presence! If I go up to heaven, you are there; if I go down to the grave, you are there. If I ride the wings of the morning, if I dwell by the farthest oceans, even there your hand will guide me, and your strength will support me" (Psalm 139:7–9, NLT).

Where could I go, and why would I want to? Thank you, Father, for refusing to leave me, despite my sins, my wandering, my mistakes, and all my imperfections. I can mess up so badly, "Yet I still belong to you, you hold my right hand. You guide me with your counsel, leading me to a glorious destiny. Whom have I in heaven but you? I desire you more than anything on earth. My health may fail, and my spirit may grow weak, but God remains the strength of my heart; He is mine forever" (Psalm 73:23–26, NLT). Amen.

Thank you, God.
Love,
Me

Where Could I Go?

The whole idea of abiding in God's presence, staying within his watchful gaze and his protective hand, rang true for me one night in a very real way. I just have to smile as I look back on the experience that taught me this, and I think, *Wow! There's just no getting away from him!*

Years ago, I was in a very bad car accident. It could have been fatal—except my Father was there. Thank God for his presence that night and his angels, as well. "For he orders his angels to protect you wherever you go" (Psalm 91:11, TLB). My mom used to read Psalm 91 to my sister and me, every morning before school, and whenever she got in the car to drive anywhere, she would recite it. It became as familiar to me as the Pledge of Allegiance. I'm grateful for that, and I too have made it my promise to claim every morning and every time I get behind the wheel. Ever since I was a little girl, I have held onto the words in this Psalm. I don't like starting my day, or going anywhere, before first establishing and claiming my Father's protective promises.

And the night of my accident, they held true. I was alone in my vehicle when I came to. I didn't know, for the first few minutes, where I was or what had happened. Once I realized that I was in my truck, I tried opening the door to get out, but it was jammed in. I was trapped inside, and for some reason, I thought I had driven off the road and landed in a lake or something (one of my biggest fears). I thought that was why I couldn't get out. I was terrified! But when I saw that the window was completely broken, I reached my arm out and realized that the cold night air surrounded me, not water. For a moment, I was relieved—that is, until I touched my face.

As the realization that I was in a car accident began to sink in, I put my hand to my cheek and felt shards of glass all over the side of my face. I began screaming. I tried crawling out of the broken window, but I couldn't get out. My legs were pinned beneath the steering wheel that was crushed down pretty low, and I was stuck. It was all I could do to try and stretch my neck far enough out the window to scream and hope someone would hear me. I didn't know where I was or if I was in danger of another car crashing into me. I didn't know if I was in the middle of the road or the middle of a cornfield for that matter.

A few seconds later, two ladies ran up to me and assured me that help was coming. And before I knew it, the ambulance showed up. Turns out, I was in the middle of the intersection I had just blown through. In my tiredness (after teaching all day and then waitressing that night), I had failed to stop at a blinking red light. I totaled my truck and someone else's van.

The firemen got out the "jaws of life" and pulled me from my crushed vehicle. The paramedics put me on a stretcher and into the ambulance. We were on our way to the hospital when I started to become more aware of the circumstances surrounding my accident. I remembered that I had just ended my shift at the restaurant where I worked, the nights my son was at his dad's. I was a "closer" that night, so it was really late. One of the paramedics started talking to me about all of that, and I was able to recall things and answer his questions. While we talked, he was looking through my purse, trying to find identification.

As soon as he found my driver's license, he said, "Josephine Tripoli? Oh, you're Joe Tripoli's daughter!" He immediately made that connection and was extra kind to me simply because he knew whose daughter I was. In our small town, everyone knows my dad.

Really, where can I go from his presence? Everywhere I go, people know him. Even in that ambulance in the middle of the night, my dad was "with me." To me, that night perfectly exemplified how we cannot escape our loving Father's presence.

> Where can I go from your Spirit?
> Where can I flee from your presence?
> If I go to the heavens, you are there;
> if I make my bed in the depths, you are there;
> If I rise on the wings of the dawn,
> if I settle on the far side of the sea,

even there your hand will guide me,
your right hand will hold me fast. (Psalm 139:7–10, NIV)

Yet I am always with you;
you hold me by my right hand.
You guide me with your counsel,
and afterward you will take me into glory.
Whom have I in heaven but you?
And earth has nothing I desire besides you.
My flesh and my heart may fail,
but God is the strength of my heart
and my portion forever. (Psalm 73:23–26, NIV)

Lord, to whom would we go? (John 6:68, NLT)

Trust in the Lord with all your heart
And lean not on your own understanding;
In all your ways submit to Him,
And He will make your paths straight. (Proverbs 3:5–6, NIV)

To Whom Would I Run?

In all things,
I lean not
on my own understanding.

Lord…
I have no understanding.
I don't understand
how the best made plans
can be trashed,
the highest hopes dashed,
and two lives
once joined,
fatally crashed.

And so…
to whom would I go?
On whom would I lean?
Myself?
Lord, I've proven how weak
I am.

Would I lean on a man…
his promises?
They've all failed,
those "treasures" sunk,
those ships
sailed.

Lord, to whom would I go?
To whom would I run…
than to my loving Father,
and His beloved Son.

There

I believe God asked me the question, "Are you going to take your life with you, or are you going to leave it there?" You know where "there" is. Each of us probably has our own definition of "there." It's that place we left our heart. It's those memories we wish we could stop remembering. It's that hurt we wish we would stop feeling. "There."

God,

I don't know.

    I *want* to leave that place and go forward. But you're right (of course, you are), I can't go anywhere as long as my life is there. Oh, I can walk around, go to work, and take care of things. I can function, but not live. Help me, Father, I can't seem to stop residing in my past.

    God, only you know and feel my emptiness, and it's because I haven't taken my life with me. I've left it there. So I am, in essence, living deprived of life. I don't want to keep walking around, pretending to be fine, but being empty. I want to take my life with me, not leave it behind. I don't want to live my life lifeless anymore.

Love,
Me

Lifeless

I can love you all I want
but if you're not for real,
I'm still left wanting.

I can love you with all my heart
but if you're not for real,
I'll still have an empty heart.

I can need you like the air I breathe
but if you're not for real,
I'll still gasp for every breath.

I can hold onto you with all my might
but if you're not for real,
I'm still left with open arms.

I can convince you of how you should love me
but if you're not for real,
I'll never feel it.

I can put all my hope in you
but if you're not for real,
I will sink within myself.

I can live my life for you
but if you're not for real,
I'll become lifeless.

The problem is,
you're not
for real.

So I can't love you
or breathe you

or hold you
or convince you.
I can't put my hope in you
or live for you.

Because
I will not be left wanting
Or empty
Or breathless…
And I can't sink any lower,
And I won't live my life
lifeless
anymore.

Dear God,

You know I'm not talking about you in that poem. You are for real. You would never leave me feeling lifeless, for you are the Creator of life. I wrote that poem years ago when I wasn't putting you first, a time when I looked to someone, other than you, to fulfill my life. It was my own fault, no one else's.

And look what happens when we do that—we're left lifeless. We cannot build our lives around anyone but you. When we try, we quickly find out no one can live up to that expectation or be our source of life. That position is yours alone. Forgive me, Father, for making that mistake and keep me from repeating it. And please, now help me to move on. Heal me. Free me from this pain. I want to pick up my life and move forward. Even this book is an attempt to do that—to go on and make something good come from something painful.

So to answer your question, Father, no, I'm not going to leave my life there. I'm going to take it with me and live it.

Love,
Me

Chains

Liquid chains
Wrapped 'round my soul,
Making their mark,
Taking their toll.
Flowing
Ebbing
Streams of tears,
Coiling,
Crippling
Me with fears.
Breathing
Seething
Collapsing
Binding…
Always losing,
Never finding.
How could I snap
What wouldn't break?
The tears
Wouldn't cease,
The fear
Wouldn't shake.
I couldn't do it—
It had to be You.
I wouldn't have made it—
It had to be through.

Have you ever felt "chains" like that before? Have you felt crippled by your own thoughts, choked by your own tears? It's hard to break free from these chains because they never stop flowing, moving, twisting. They're not made of iron—that would be easier to break. Someone, somewhere, has got a tool for that. But there's no tool, not even in my dad's giant toolbox, that could cut through my chains of tears—those chains, linked together by painful memories. And it seems like the harder I tried, the more I squirmed around trying to untangle myself, the tighter those chains got, and the more bound I was by them. That's why I wrote, "I couldn't do it. It had to be you." Only God, in his all-knowing and all-powerful strength, can break us free—free from every kind of chain.

He's bigger and stronger than anything else that holds you. But if you don't go to him, you'll never break free. You will become a slave to anything else you go to for your freedom. Anything else that you let wrap itself around you will control you and constrict you until you're lifeless.

I'm not saying to live a solitary life because anything other than God will strangle you. No! God calls us to be his people and a reflection of his love to the world. You can't live, let alone love, in isolation. We are to love and reach out to others. In fact, the Bible tells us we are to be "the hands and feet of Christ."

Just don't put anything else above him! "Dear children, keep away from anything that might take God's place in your hearts" (1 John 5:21, NLT). He deserves first place in your heart and in your life, and as long as he is first, then there is a place for everything else that he wants to give you. "But seek first the Kingdom of God and his righteousness, and all these things will be added to you" (Matthew 6:33, ESV).

If you're feeling the way I was, just ask your Father to free you and work *with* him. Allow him to come in and begin the untangling process. Simply tell him you're not strong enough to break those chains yourself, but you know he is. He knows exactly what is holding you captive. He knows what those chains are made of. He was there, and his own heart broke as he watched you let yourself be bound and sold into slavery.

But he doesn't intend on letting you stay there. God wants to reclaim you as his own, as his child, not a slave. It is not his will that you be a slave to anything. "For this is what the Lord says, 'You were sold for nothing, and without money you will be redeemed'" (Isaiah 52:3). And once he has redeemed you, you will finally break free from those chains and experience the freedom you were made to live in, the freedom Christ died to give you. "If the Son sets you free, you will be free indeed" (John 8:36, NIV).

> The Spirit of the Lord God is upon me, because the Lord has anointed me to bring good news to the poor. He has sent me to comfort the brokenhearted and to proclaim that captives will be released and prisoners will be freed. (Isaiah 61:1, ESV)

I keep praying and trusting in God, and I know he won't fail me. Sometimes becoming free is a process rather than an instant miracle. Be patient. God, in his infinite wisdom, sometimes works with us in layers. First of all, the thing that has bound us may be buried very deep by now. It may take a gradual process of uncovering hurts and deceptions that we've bought into before God can get to the root of our bondage.

Have you ever tried to untangle a necklace, especially a delicate one? Sometimes it can get so tied up in knots that you're afraid it might just break if you attempt to straighten it out. Well, that's what our lives can get like. Our lives are very delicate and can be easily twisted and broken. God might not want to just yank on it. He doesn't want to break us; he wants to fix us. It might take some careful lifting up of layers, one at a time, to get to the main knot and untie it. But when he does, no matter how long that takes, we will be restored and shine like new. "Behold, I make all things new" (Revelation 21:5, KJV).

Another reason your freedom might not come instantly is because God wants to teach you something really important in the process of healing you so that you won't find yourself in bondage again to the same things over and over. We're human, and he knows it. We tend to repeat the same mistakes in our lives, go around the same mountains, so to speak. Why? Because we haven't yet learned from our mistakes. We think we have, but as soon as God gets us out of one mess, we fall (or jump) into another. As soon as he breaks the chains around our wrists, we hold out our arms and let someone, or something else, put new chains on us and lead us away yet again.

God doesn't want that. He wants you to be free and to never go back into captivity (whatever that captivity looks like for you—it's not from him). God told the Israelites, as they were wandering around their mountain and were tempted to sell themselves back into slavery, "You must never return to Egypt" (Deuteronomy 17:16, NLT). He knows that we're creatures of habit and that sometimes we want to go back to a bad thing because it's at least familiar. It may be painful, even humiliating, but it's what we're used to. It has become our home, and it's just too hard to pack up and move on.

But God has so much more for us than that! Therefore, he may not just snap your chains off and set you loose to run back to whatever it is he knows you'll run back to. Instead, he will work with you in such a way that you will learn what he wants to reveal to you about yourself. And when you finally release your weaknesses to him, then he can truly heal and deliver you once and for all. "Therefore, dear brothers and sisters, you have no obligation to do what your sinful nature urges you to do" (Romans 8:12, NLT). You can be done with that; you do not have to keep falling into the same traps.

It is possible. Don't believe the lie that's telling you that you could never be free from your chains. God is a chain-breaker. That's what he does. He has done it for countless others, and he will do it for you. Remember he is a perfect Father, and he does not have favorites. "God is no respecter of persons" (Acts 10:34). The New American Standard Bible puts it this way, "God is not one to show partiality." Come to him, knots and all, and let him untangle your mess, straighten your life, and restore you to the brilliance in which he created you.

Lastly, this process may take time because God wants a relationship with you. That is more important to him than your knots. Remember he already sees you as beautiful; you already sparkle in his eyes. But your chains keep you from knowing how beautiful you are and from knowing the life you could have. They keep you from enjoying the abundant life Jesus died to give you. In John 10:10, Jesus says, "I have come that they may have life, and have it to the full."

So if you don't feel like you're living life "to the full," then pursue a relationship with your heavenly Father. If you've already got a relationship with him, get closer. Through the process of him untangling your mess and healing you, your relationship with him will grow and be strengthened, and that's what he desires the most. That's also what you need the most in order to live an abundant life.

You can trust him to do this. He won't leave you to figure it all out by yourself. He wants a relationship with you. Put your hope and trust in him; he will not fail you. "I will never fail you, I will never abandon you" (Hebrews 13:5, NLT). Maybe other people have failed you time and time again. Maybe everybody else has disappointed you or even abandoned you, but God won't. Maybe you're afraid to get your hopes up or to put your trust in someone, but God is worthy of your trust, even if no one else is. You can put your hope in him and not be afraid of being let down. "Be strong, and let your heart take courage, all you who hope in the Lord" (Psalm 31:24, NASB).

Don't give up. Keep seeking him and keep drawing closer. The more you seek him, the more you'll find him. Never stop looking to him and for him in everything, and in everything, he'll show up. You'll start to live your life *with* him, in his presence, and you'll find your beautiful life of freedom.

> And so I tell you, keep on asking, and you will receive what you ask for. Keep seeking, and you will find. Keep on knocking and the door will be opened to you. For everyone who asks, receives. Everyone who seeks, finds. And to everyone who knocks, the door will be opened. (Luke 11:9–10, NLT)

Don't Look Back

As I pray to be set free from the pain of my past, I am reminded of the story of Lot's wife. In Genesis 19, the story is told of how the angel of the Lord came to Lot and his family to rescue them and set them free before he destroyed the terrible and sinful place in which they lived.

> When Lot hesitated, the angels seized his hand and the hands of his wife and two daughters and rushed them to safety outside the city, for the Lord was merciful. When they were safely out of the city, one of the angels ordered, "Run for your lives! And don't look back or stop anywhere in the valley! Escape to the mountains, or you will be swept away."… But Lot's wife looked back as she was following behind him, and she turned into a pillar of salt. (Genesis 19:16–17,26, NLT)

Sometimes God has to literally force us to leave a bad place or toxic situation. We don't always want to leave our prison because to us, it might be home. However, when I read the angel's instructions, I hear the following four very specific commands if we are to be free and not swept away:

- Run for your life.
- Don't look back.
- Don't stop in the valley.
- Escape to the mountains.

First of all, he commands them to run, not walk. He didn't tell Lot to take his time, talk it over with his wife, or even think about it. There is a definite sense of urgency here, as there should be any time we are surrounded by sin. We are to run from sin! The Bible tells us to run from the very appearance of evil (1 Thessalonians 5:22). Being in sin is a life-and-death situation. Don't linger in it. Get the heck out—and fast! He said, "Run for your lives." Their very lives depended on how fast they got out of there. It's no different for you and me. When we find ourselves in a situation of moral decay, when sin surrounds us, then we are not where we're supposed to be. Don't take sin lightly! The Bible is clear, "For the wages of sin is death" (Romans 6:23, KJV). Run!

Secondly he says, "Don't look back." Again, it's a clear message. If you want to enter into the freedom God has for you, don't turn around and look back. Look in the direction you're going, or you're never going to get there.

Believe me, I'm preaching to myself here. I can have a hard time walking away. I can focus so much on my past, on regrets, or the way I wish life would have gone. Sometimes I just want another chance to go back and do things better this time. I wish I could go back and make smarter decisions. I wish I could go back and not act so self-ishly. I wish I could go back and tell someone I love them one more time, or thank them, or say I'm sorry. But I can't.

I was dwelling in past one day, not too long ago, and God spoke to me and said, "Don't be like Lot's wife."

I don't want to be like her; she turned into a pillar of salt! Now I've been accused of reading too much into stuff before, so I don't mind if that's what you think, but here's what I think. Salt, here, can symbol-ize tears. Maybe I'm not going to turn into a pillar of salt, but I might just turn into a big puddle of tears if I keep looking back! I might just "cry myself to death," if I don't turn around and face forward. I know, as well as you do, that there's no future in the past. "Remember not the former things, nor consider the things of old. Behold, I am doing a new thing; now it springs forth, do you not perceive it?" (Isaiah 43:18–19, ESV).

The next instruction given by the angel is, "Don't stop in the valley." A valley represents a low point. For goodness' sake, don't stop at a low point! We've all been there—a low point in our lives—but that's the last place we should stop and rest or set up camp! Depression is down there! A victim mentality is down there! The longer you linger, the harder it'll be to climb up out of it. If you're feeling low, then keep on moving; you can rest later. Just get out of the valley. Don't stop until you've reached higher ground, and then you can rest for a while.

Higher ground—that leads us to the angel's final command. "Escape to the mountains." How often does God speak of his holy mountain? A lot. It is his dwelling place. He wants us to abide with him there. Way back in the days of Moses, God lived among his people and spoke to them from the mountain. King David refers to this mountain often in his writing. "Who may climb the mountain of the Lord and enter where he lives?" (Psalm 24:3, TLB). So if you want to abide with God, you have to climb that mountain.

Now, even if you've never physically climbed a real mountain before, you know it's hard! It would take strength and extreme determination. Well, climbing the mountain of God is no different. It's not easy! You have to continuously take higher ground, leaving the lower, lesser, places (and things) behind you. Yes, you're going to fall sometimes. Yes, you may get weak and feel discouraged; you may think you're never going to make it. But keep getting up, keep climbing; you don't want to settle for anything less than a life lived with God. It wouldn't be worth it, settling never is. It's never what you wanted. Climb his mountain, escape into his presence. Only there will you find freedom and an abundant life.

I believe that the angel's advice to Lot and his family holds true for us today. Jesus came to give us a full life and an open road. And the only time we should glance in our rearview mirror is to humbly remember where we've been so as not to return. "I came that they may have life and have it abundantly" (John 10:10, ESV). The devil, on the other hand, has the opposite purpose and agenda. "The thief comes only to steal and kill and destroy" (John 10:10, ESV).

So, what direction are you facing? If all you can see is a life robbed of its joy, a life that looks destroyed, then you can be pretty sure not only of the direction you're facing, but also whose face you're staring into. Are you facing fire and torment, fear, lies, depression, and hopelessness? Then guess who you're looking at, and for God's sake, turn around! Stop looking back; it will be the end of you—salt, tears, however it comes, it'll be the end.

A defeated life and a certain death is all the devil has for you. It's all he could possibly offer. So take your eyes off your enemy and get them back on your Savior! Do you want your life saved, turned around, and renewed? Then face the only One who can do it! And believe me, he's not waiting for you in your past. He's in your present, and he wants to lead you, by the hand, into a glorious future.

See his grace, his love for you, and his forgiveness. It's not the reluctant forgiveness we sometimes offer each other. You know what I mean, "Well, okay, I guess I can forgive you… but…" No, he's not like that! He can't wait to forgive you! You don't have to talk him into it. He already shed his blood for just that purpose. You don't have to try to convince him that you deserve his forgiveness because you don't; none of us deserve that kind of mercy. But he offers it anyway. He gives it simply because he loves you. His is a joyful, willing, excited-to-give-it kind of forgiveness.

When you look up and turn around, you'll see him and the direction in which he wants to take you. He will lead you and guide you, step by step if you'll let him, into your future, your abundant life, and your eternal salvation.

> Turn us again to yourself, O Lord God of Heaven's Armies. Make your face shine down upon us. Only then will we be saved. (Psalm 80:19, NLT)

Return to Me

Oh, return to me, for I have paid the price to set you free.

—Isaiah 44:22 (TLB)

Did your dad ever help you get out of some trouble? Maybe you got involved in a bad situation, the wrong crowd, or you made mistakes and when it came time to pay the price, you couldn't. You were stuck with, or just beat up by, your own choices, and you felt like you really messed things up beyond repair. Have you ever been there and had someone (maybe your dad, maybe not) step in and fix what you broke, pay what you couldn't afford, or pick you up? Maybe someone simply reminded you, "It's okay. Life's not over." I think all of us can relate to getting into trouble, but maybe not all of us can relate to having someone intervene.

Maybe no one has ever come through for you. You've been "drowning" for years, and no one has ever thrown you a rope. I know you feel alone. In your eyes, you are, have always been, and will always be on your own. *But you can't see everything!* You don't see the way your heavenly Father has saved you from things that he never let happen, and so you don't even know about them because he spared you. Whether you see him in your life or not, he is, has always been, and will always be there.

He hasn't saved you from everything though. He gives us free will. Sometimes we make wrong choices. Sometimes we wind up in trouble, not because of our own choices, but because of someone else's. And sometimes we end up in trouble or suffering due to no one's choices at all. Things just happen—sad and unfair tragedy and misfortune. It's all part of this life on earth. We live in a broken world

67

where bad things happen, even to good people. So when I talk about being in a bad place, please realize I am not implying that you got yourself there.

You may have gone through, or are now going through, things that you did not ask for, and pain you do not deserve. You may be living through a situation that you wouldn't wish on your worst enemy. But if you're reading this, then you still have breath left in you, and so he has saved you (perhaps countless times) from death. You're still here. It's not over. If you are alive, it's because he's kept you alive—and for a good reason. Your story is not finished.

However, if you're not looking at your life from that perspective, then you may actually think that God hasn't rescued you, but rather abandoned you. Don't believe that lie any longer. You see, he would never leave you. Even if you had poor examples of parents in your life, even if other people who were supposed to love you left you, you can be assured that God's not like that. "Even if my father and mother abandon me, the Lord will hold me close" (Psalm 27:10, NLT).

Your heavenly Father will never leave you, his own heart couldn't take it. In fact, his heart breaks and breaks the further and further you get from him. He wants to step in and save you. He wants to rescue you from the trouble you've found yourself in (no matter how you got there) and he wants to comfort and restore your soul.

He cried out to his people, Israel, when they walked away from him, and he loves us no less. He begged them, "'Put all your rebellion behind you, and find yourselves a new heart and a new spirit. For why should you die, O people of Israel? I don't want you to die,' says the Sovereign Lord. 'Turn back and live!'" (Ezekiel 18:31–32, NLT).

He paid the price to set you free. That implies the fact that until he saves you, you are not free. You are in bondage to whatever you fell into, or stepped into, when you stepped away from him. Again, I don't mean this to be a judgmental statement; it may not be your fault, it's just a fact of life down here. We all fall or step away sometimes. And every time we step away from our heavenly Father, we step into a prison. And it takes his sacrifice—the price he paid—to free us again. If it were not for the blood of Christ shed upon the cross for you and me, we would all be eternally imprisoned, never to be set free, because there is no other way. Only Jesus, in his perfect love, could and would and did pay our debt.

Our Father begs us to return to him. That implies that we have all fallen away. "For all have sinned and fall short of the glory of God" (Romans 3:23, NIV). We have all, at one time or another, walked down a path that led in the wrong direction. Maybe we chose that path, maybe we got suckered into it, maybe someone held our hand and led us astray, but we've all walked there. Doesn't matter, he wants us back. He knows the mistakes we've made, the traps we've fallen into, or continue to fall into, and he wants us back. He knows how desperate we are for him, even if we don't know it, or won't acknowledge it. And still, he pleads with us, "Return to me."

He knows we can't do it on our own and that we are completely dependent on him. That's okay. That's by his design. Remember he wants a relationship with you. He wants you to be continually and completely dependent on him. "So now, come back to your God. Act with love and justice and always depend on him" (Hosea 12:6, NLT). Don't feel like you have to get yourself strong enough first before returning to him. His strength is made complete in your weakness, and his grace is sufficient to cover you. "My grace is sufficient for you, and my strength is made perfect in your weakness" (2 Corinthians 12:9, NKJV). Just turn to him and let him do the rest.

Why is this so hard for us? As children, it should be easier to depend on our Father than what we make it. Why do we resist this rest, this love? Maybe it's immaturity. Maybe it's rebellion or selfishness. Maybe it's disbelief, because if we *really* believed that we could rush back into our Father's arms and just lean on and depend on him, we would do it in a heartbeat! Wouldn't we?

Not once (I can't find it anywhere in the Bible) does God say, "You made your bed. Now lie in it." Your parents may have used that logic on you, but he won't. *Come here. I still love you. Turn around. Come back. I forgive you. Return to me. I still love you. Come here. Turn around. I forgive you. I still love you.* He never stops calling. So long as you're on this earth, you can still turn around and run back into the open arms of your Father.

He keeps calling to us for as long as it takes for us to listen. As often as we repeat our mistakes, he repeats his invitation: *Just come here. I forgive you. I still love you. I can get you out of this. Trust me. I know you think you're in over your head this time, but it's nothing to me. I'll move mountains for you. I'll do whatever it takes. I love you. Oh, return to me.* I can almost hear him now as I think about his undying, untiring love for us.

No one else is ever going to love us like that! No one could! He won't give up. He'll call to us our whole lives. But the quicker we listen, the quicker our lives are going to make sense again, and the more fulfilled they will be. So why wait?

Open your Bible and see how many times he calls us to return to him. Read his promises that he longs to fulfill for us. The following are just a few:

> Only in returning to me and resting in me will you be saved. (Isaiah 30:15, NLT)

> So the Lord must wait for you to come to him so he can show you his love and compassion. For the Lord is a faithful God. (Isaiah 30:18, NLT)

> "My wayward children," says the Lord, "come back to me, and I will heal your hearts." (Jeremiah 3:22, NLT)

> I will watch over and care for them, and I will bring them back here again. I will build them up and not tear them down. I will plant them and not uproot them. I will give them hearts that recognize me as the Lord. They will be my people, and I will be their God, for they will return to me wholeheartedly. (Jeremiah 24:6–7, NLT)

> Return, O Israel, to the Lord your God, for your sins have brought you down. Bring your confes-

sions and return to the Lord. Say to him, "Forgive all our sins and graciously receive us, so that we may offer you praises." The Lord says, "Then I will heal you of your faithlessness; my love will know no bounds, my anger will be gone forever." (Hosea 14:1–2,4, NLT)

Don't tear your clothing in your grief but tear your hearts instead. Return to the Lord your God, for he is merciful and compassionate, slow to anger and filled with unfailing love. He is eager to relent and not punish. (Joel 2:13, NLT)

He understands that sometimes we want to turn to him, but we need help with even that. We don't know where to begin. Remember he won't leave you to figure it all out on your own. All you have to do is ask him. Tell him you can't do it on your own and ask him to turn you around. Our Father loves when we seek his help. He's a good Father. He doesn't roll his eyes and sigh, "Again?" No. He honors our humility and desires our dependence. So don't feel bad about needing him to help you turn around. Even King David prayed this prayer, "Turn us again to yourself, O God. Make your face shine down upon us. Only then will we be saved" (Psalm 80:3, NLT). Make this your daily prayer and watch him turn your life around.

A Father's Compassion

"For the mountains may depart and the hills be removed, but my steadfast love shall not depart from you, and my covenant of peace shall not be removed," says the Lord who has compassion on you.
—Isaiah 54:10 (ESV)

You've known people who just seem to have a big heart; well, no one has a bigger heart than God! His heart is overwhelmingly full of compassion and love for us.

Now, we all know what it's like to seek and expect compassion from others and then not get it. We beg for their compassion only to be let down. It shocks the soul when people, especially people we love and who we thought loved us, show us no compassion. Often it's those we trusted the most, gave our hearts to, who let us down the most.

Even King David realized this anguish. "It was not an enemy who taunted me—then I could have borne it; I could have hidden and escaped. But it was you, a man like myself, my companion and my friend" (Psalm 55:12–13, TLB). I know what it's like to feel utterly alone and up against a mountain of betrayal, rejected and completely hopeless. Have you been there too? You're living in survival mode, barely breathing, and just an ounce of compassion—from anyone—would go a long way. It would make all the difference in the world.

It's hard to believe how people, imperfect as we all are, in the same boat so to speak, cannot afford one another the compassion we need, yet our perfect and holy God can and does. That is "Amazing

Grace" if I ever knew it! And it does make all the difference in the world.

Dear Father,

Thank you for your love and compassion. I know I couldn't survive this life without it. I don't think anyone could. Thank you for always getting me and knowing how I feel, and even when I'm wrong, still having compassion on me. Teach me to treat others with that same compassion. None of us deserve it, Lord, but if *you* can still offer it, then surely we can.

It's not about being right or wrong. It's about being kind. Having compassion doesn't mean condoning sin. You don't condone sin, yet you are still compassionate. Help us to follow your lead here, and teach us how to do the same with the people in our lives. Show us how to offer compassion and bring your peace to this heartbroken world.

Love,
Me

Broken Wing

When someone hurts me, I get real "tough." Yeah, I might cry like a baby at first, even throw some childish tantrums, but then something happens. Something stops me, something clicks, and then I get mad. I feel myself pull up my bootstraps, and get ready for a fight. I'm going to defend myself at all costs. Whoever hurt me is going to know, in no uncertain terms, "You won't do this to me again."

I'm not saying this works. I'm just saying that's how I tend to operate (when guided by my own self-serving will). I will work very hard to convince, not only my offender, but also myself that "I'm done," and that I will no longer be walked on. Maybe it's just my way of comforting or reassuring myself, *It's okay. I'm not going to let this happen again. Don't worry. I can take care of myself!* And then I can hide behind this assertiveness (I think that's what the world calls it nowadays) and crumble inside.

Because no matter how hard you get on the outside, your attitude, your demeanor, your words—on the inside, your spirit stays just as fragile as the day you were born. It's like the little you. Do you even remember who that is? The you before the world, and people, changed you. The real you before you grew up, before life happened. Your spirit.

God created it, he breathed it into you, so it doesn't change—it's you. It doesn't listen to the voices, like maybe your brain does to "get real." (In fact, it is more real and true than any other part of you.) It doesn't listen to the voices that say, "Toughen up!" It can't.

Notice I didn't say it can't be strong. It's the strongest part of you there is. I'm just implying that it can't be calloused into becoming what the world would make it. It won't be weathered by the storms of this life like your body, maybe even your soul. Your spirit is different.

It's God's life breathed into you. Your spirit can't be fake, or destroyed by others and their opinions. It can only be true. It can only be you.

I think it may grow weak at times, even get hurt (because of its innocence), but not killed. The spirit that God breathed into you is stronger than whatever comes against it. "My flesh and my heart may fail, but God is the strength of my heart and my portion forever" (Psalm 73:26, NIV). God is the strength of your heart. (Some translations use "spirit" for "heart.") He remains, and therefore, so does the spirit he put in you when he first created you.

I'm also not saying it can't get buried beneath stuff that happens or even stomped on, but it survives. If you're like me, you may feel like your spirit has been trampled upon. You might feel like roadkill. It may seem like your spirit is buried so deep beneath your burdens that it'll never get up, let alone speak up, ever again. And while it may lie silent, crushed, and exhausted, it's only exhausted from fighting so hard. Your spirit's a survivor, and will rise up again, and lead you back to the truth of who you are, who God uniquely created you to be and always be.

> For you created in my inmost being; you knit me together in my mother's womb. I praise you because I am fearfully and wonderfully made; your works are wonderful, I know that full well. (Psalm 139:13–14, NIV)

During a very difficult and sad time in my life, I had a dream of all this rubble lying everywhere. The setting looked like an old temple with stones, pillars, and the like, all knocked down, broken, and lying in ruins. Everything was shattered. A complete mess. If it was a temple, or whatever it was at one time, it was now just a pile of wasted material. Whatever structure may have given it beauty in its day was gone—it was barely recognizable. What once was magnificent was now desolate.

Then slowly, out from underneath the heaps of rubble, a tiny baby bird, barely able to move, inched its way out. It looked half alive. It struggled just to move. (Now remember, this is a dream, so it doesn't have to make perfect sense.) Then I noticed that it was walking on little wooden crutches, and one of its wings was wrapped in a tiny white sling. It was crushed and beaten, but not destroyed.

I just saw it for a second, and then I woke up. But I immediately knew that the little bird represented me—my spirit. It was badly injured, it was shaken, it was broken, but it was still there. It didn't die even though, so many times, I would have sworn it did. It was taking a while, but it was slowly making its way out from underneath the heaping mess, that was my life. Pushing past the broken walls, limping away with a broken wing—that's me. That is you. That is all of us.

See how much stronger we are than we give ourselves credit? It's not about being tough or hard; it's about being strong and true. The spirit that God breathed into you from the very beginning is who you really are, and that spirit is powerful! "Tiny but mighty!" I have to laugh because my parents used to always call me that—tiny but mighty—when I was a little girl (funny how those things stick).

The problem is we live in a fallen world, and it's easy to feel "tiny," but not so easy to feel "mighty." There are huge heaps of ruins all around us. We fall, we crash, we get buried, we rise, we fall...it's part of our human existence here in this world. It's a mess down here, and we have a very real enemy.

The devil will relentlessly try to trip you up, deceive you, push you around, and bury you if you let him. That's right—if you let him. The Word says, "Submit yourselves, then, to God. Resist the devil, and he will flee from you" (James 4:7, NIV). It is a daily battle, but you have to submit yourself to your heavenly Father, and you have to actively resist the devil. You cannot be passive about this, or he will not flee, and you will be swept away and buried.

I said the devil will relentlessly try to destroy you; I didn't say he will succeed—that is up to you. You see, he is an already defeated foe. He was defeated and disarmed at the cross by Jesus Christ, the Lamb of God. Satan has no power over you that you don't give him; and you don't have to give him anything! His power over you was taken from him when Jesus took your sins upon himself, died, and rose again. However, the devil will still try to use anyone or anything he can to knock you off your feet, break your heart, and crush your spirit. He comes to do nothing less than destroy you. Remember, "The thief comes only to steal and kill and destroy" (John 10:10, ESV). Your enemy wants to bury you. But you don't have to let him!

Try as he might, you belong to God! If you will but look to your Father in heaven, call upon the name of Jesus and give him your heart, he will raise you up out of the rubble, out of the mess you made, and the brokenness you've battled. He will restore your wreckage, "For the Lord comforts Zion; he comforts all her waste places" (Isaiah 51:3, ESV). He will mend your wounds and comfort your heart. He is near to us who are crushed in spirit. "The Lord is close to the brokenhearted; he rescues those whose spirits are crushed" (Psalm 34:18, NLT).

The devil can cause quite a mess, but God knows how to "clean house!" And you are the temple of the Holy Spirit; your body is a house for the Lord to dwell in. "Don't you realize that your body is the temple of the Holy Spirit, who lives in you and was given to you by God?" (1 Corinthians 6:19, NLT). The Holy Spirit will cleanse and comfort your heart if you submit to him.

How do you do that? Don't harden your heart when walls come crashing down around you, and people hurl their words at you like stones. Instead, take those hurts, all that pain and damage, to your Comforter. Ask him to heal you and to keep you from bitterness. Ask him to help you forgive those who hurt you. He already knows you need his help with this. No one can do it on their own. Just reaffirm your trust in him and cast all your cares upon him. "Give all your worries and cares to God, for he cares about you" (1 Peter 5:7, NLT).

You see, the enemy can't win, can't destroy you, or even get to you if you refuse to allow him into your heart. Refuse to allow him to harden your heart. Refuse to allow him to embitter your heart. Instead, allow God to soften your heart. Allow God to mold your heart. Allow God to mend your heart. It's not automatic. It takes humility and forgiveness, and those things take time and a willingness to submit to God's will over your own. But it will be so worth it!

Don't you want him to restore and revive you? Don't you want to crawl out from underneath what other people have done to you, and the shadows they have cast over your life? Don't you want to be free and no longer subjected to them and the damage they did? Don't you want to remember what it feels like to be you again? Don't you want to emerge from that mess, throw aside those crutches, take the sling off, and fly once more? Then let him heal your broken wings by choosing to forgive.

Soar

Locked in sorrow,
Bound in words…
Even the prettiest cage,
Is no place for birds.

Humility
Unlatched the hook,
Forgiveness
Opened the door.
Yeah, I fell on my face,
Before learning how to soar.

It hasn't been easy,
Finding a place to land…
But when the storm rages,
He holds out His hand.

So I'll take refuge,
Where my heart can be free…
Peace
In the storm,
Just His hand and me.

Don't Hurt Back

I was getting ready one morning, and God told me, "Don't hurt back." It was as clear as day. If you've ever been struck by a bit of divine wisdom, you know it's real because it stops you in your tracks with its simple profoundness. With me, it's usually an inaudible word from within my spirit that just seems so right that there's no way it's from me. It's so simple that I always think, *Yeah, why didn't I think of that?* Hmm, because I couldn't.

That's just it, you and I could never think of something that doesn't come from the human mind and our limited understanding. If we could, it wouldn't be so wonderful—it wouldn't be *divine*. I don't know about you, but I'm not often impressed by my own thoughts. However, I am amazed at the thoughts of God! "How precious to me are your thoughts, God!" (Psalm 139:17, NIV).

"Don't hurt back" was the thought he shared with me that morning. I think it goes back to what I was talking about before, you know, not letting the enemy harden your heart, but rather letting God soften and mold it. Part of that, I think, is not always being ready for a fight. When someone hurts us, it's our natural tendency to want to retaliate. Someone says something mean to you, you say something mean to them (or about them). Someone rejects you, you reject them back. Someone makes you feel stupid, you make them feel stupid. It's childish really. But not the way children of God should act. Our Father taught us better! We need to grow up! "But I say, love your enemies! Pray for those who persecute you. In that way, you will be acting as true children of your Father in heaven" (Matthew 5:44–45, NLT).

Again, I think it boils down to forgiveness. You can choose to forgive or to hurt back, but choosing the latter will hurt you more in the long run. Forgiveness is a daily choice. Some people devastate us so badly that even though we want to forgive more than anything, it just feels impossible. But thank God, forgiveness does not depend on our feelings, or else we'd hardly ever be able to forgive (or be forgiven for that matter).

You can still feel whatever emotion you're feeling, but choose to push past it enough to say, "God, I forgive them anyway. Help my feelings to come along, I know it might take time, but I don't want to wait to forgive. So I forgive now, and I trust you to comfort my heart and work on my emotions so I don't have to feel this way forever. I choose to forgive, Lord. Help me with this, like everything else, I can't do it on my own."

Can you just pray that prayer, no matter how you feel? It'll at least be the first step, and if you have to repeat that step every day, then do it. No matter how long it takes, don't quit forgiving. When Jesus' disciple Peter asked him how many times he should forgive someone who had sinned against him, Jesus answered, "Seventy-seven times" (Matthew 18: 21–22, NIV). I think the point Jesus was making was *as many times as it takes.*

Dear Father,

I'm sorry for acting like a child, but not a child of God. I'm sorry for not reflecting your nature especially when I get hurt. Too often, I hurt back or even just pull back, and distance myself, rather than show your love or mind your commandments. You tell us to "turn the other cheek," but more often than not, I "punch back." It's not right. I want you to treat me with mercy—that is, underserved kindness—but how can I even hope for that, if I'm not practicing it with others even in (especially in) the little things. Teach me to be more like you, Father.

Teach me how to forgive quicker and more completely. If Jesus, who is perfect and never

hurt anyone, can forgive us, who hurt him all
the time, then none of us have an excuse to hold
onto bitterness. We have no right because we've
all sinned and need forgiveness ourselves. The
quicker we forgive, the quicker we are freed from
the damage done to us, and the quicker we can
get back to living our lives. So help me, Father, to
forgive and to resist the temptation to hurt back.
And thank you for forgiving me, time and time
again. I love you.

Love,
Me

He Loved You First

Let's face it—sometimes it's hard to pray. It shouldn't be, but it can be. Sometimes I just don't know what to say anymore. But here's what I've learned. Pray anyway. You don't always have to know what to say. I mean, are you like that with anyone? Do you always know what to say? I doubt it. There are times, I think for all of us, when we're trying to communicate with someone, but we don't know what to say anymore. Why should communicating with God be any different?

Sometimes we just run out of words. Or maybe we're supposed to. Communicating isn't all about talking, you know. How often do we just quiet ourselves and wait to hear from God? Probably not often enough. Don't let being lost for words interfere with your prayer life. Words or not, spend time with your Father. Just listen. You might be given a thought or a simple word, just for you. Just spend time with him. Get close to your Father. He has everything you need and longs to provide it for you.

He already knows what you need long before you do, so just go to him and trust him as your Provider. You see, I think prayer is as much an act of humility as it is petition. It's knowing you can't do it on your own, admitting you don't have all the answers. It's acknowledging you need help and knowing where to go to get it. It's recognizing the source of everything you need and bowing before him.

Don't worry about what you're going to say or how to say it. God isn't interested in formal speeches; he just wants your heart. I'm grateful for this because sometimes I'm not sure I'm even capable of asking for the right things. I'm so glad I can still go to him though, in prayer, and just trust him. I know he'll provide whatever I need. That's it. I don't have to come up with something eloquent or even know what to ask for in order to kneel at his feet.

It's like when we were little kids. We didn't worry so much about our needs. We let our parents do that for us. Most of the time, as children, we didn't know what we needed. We may have known what we wanted, or thought we did anyway, but it's all the same—wants and needs, they were provided for us. We didn't understand them, work for them, or have to earn them; we just received them. Ah, the good ol' days!

Again, I know I have an exceptionally wonderful dad, but he knew exactly what I needed and wanted, and if it was in his power to give it to me, he did. Is that why I love him so much? No! I love him because he loves me. He's always loved me; even before my earliest memories, he was already there, taking care of me. Still today, my dad and I will go back and forth saying, "I love you," "I love you more," "No, I love you more," and then he'll settle it and win every time with, "I loved you first!"

Now, who else loves you like that? Your Father in heaven! He too loved you first, before your earliest memories, before you ever had the chance to love him back or even know him. "We love, because he first loved us" (1 John 4:19, NIV). And he loves you more and can provide far more for you than even the best dad down here, more than you could ever imagine. He is "able to do exceeding abundantly above all that we ask or think" (Ephesians 3:20). He knows your wants, and he'll exceed them. He knows your needs, and it is *always* within his power to meet them. That complete reliance on someone, like we had when we were little kids, does not have to be a thing of the past. It doesn't have to stay just a faint childhood memory. You can rely on your Father like that today!

Rest in the fact that he is your Provider, and love him because he first loved you. When you pray, make sure to thank him for taking care of you and for his promise to never stop taking care of you. Thank him for all that he has already provided and for the things yet to come. For some things, you wait in anticipation, other things you don't even know about yet, but you can still thank him because you know he's a good Father who knows how to provide for his children.

> You parents—if your children ask for a loaf of bread, do you give them a stone instead? Or if they ask for a fish, do you give them a snake? Of course not! So if you sinful people know how to give good gifts to your children, how much more will your heavenly Father give good gifts to those who ask Him. (Matthew 7:9–11, NLT)

> Ask and it will be given to you, seek and you will find; knock and the door will be opened to you. (Matthew 7:7, NIV)

No Appointment Necessary

It's important to remember you're talking to your Father. Make it real; don't make an appointment. I don't just pray at scheduled times—not that there's anything wrong with setting a designated time for daily devotion. Having a disciplined life is really important, but I never talked to my dad by appointment, so why should I talk to my Father that way? If I want to talk to my dad, I just pick up the phone and call him. It's that easy. If I want to see him, I just stop by his house and visit—no appointment necessary.

I just want to hang out with my dad. I just want to be near him and spend all the time I can with him because I love him and I want to be like him. The more time I spend with him, the more my heart is filled with love and security. The more I learn about him and his ways, the more I see myself becoming like him, more and more every day. Well, guess what? The same thing happens when we spend time and talk with our heavenly Father.

You don't think it's the same thing? It's not that easy? Yes, it is—it just takes practice. It takes time like any relationship does. It becomes natural after a while. Don't get discouraged if it doesn't feel natural at first. Most relationships don't. They take time to develop. And even those relationships that do start right off the bat only deepen and get better the more time and care we put into them.

If time and care are not put into relationships, what happens? They diminish, drift off, and eventually fall away. Believe me, you don't want that to happen to your relationship with God. You need him. And he needs you too, to fulfill the purpose for which he created you. You have an important role to play here, or else you wouldn't be here.

Did you know that when Christ died on the cross, the veil in the temple was literally torn? The barrier that separated the Holy of

Holies from the people was ripped in two. That veil was a symbol of any barrier that existed between us and the Holy God we serve, and Jesus took it away. It was torn so that now you can enter into the holy presence of your heavenly Father anytime you want. God would not have sacrificed his own beloved Son to remove the barrier between you and him if he did not desperately want to spend time with you.

> And when Jesus had cried out again in a loud voice, he gave up his spirit. At that moment the curtain of the temple was torn in two from top to bottom. The earth shook and the rocks split. (Matthew 27:50–51, NIV)

So you see, he went to great lengths to say, "Come in." You don't need to schedule an appointment with God. You don't have to wait till church on Sunday. You don't have to save your prayers for bedtime or wait until dinner to give thanks or say grace. You don't even have to wait till you clean up your act. The time is now! He's not waiting for you to be perfect or even better. He wants you now. Just like you are. Don't wait for anything to bow your heart before him, to thank him, to ask him for help, to talk to him, or just to listen.

He's been waiting, and he's always available. In fact, he wants to spend time with you more than you want to spend time with him! Seems crazy when you put it that way, but if you think about it, isn't that usually the way it goes with kids as they grow up?

Our kids grow up, and they don't think they need us anymore, they try to handle things on their own, and they forget that we're their parents. We need them as much as they need us, and we miss them. No matter how old they are or how long they've stayed away, we still just want to spend time with them; we still love them just as much.

Well, think about it. We kind of treat our heavenly Father the same way. We drift off, do our own thing, and get bogged down in our schedule and busy with life. We get overwhelmed and exhausted— too tired to spend time with him. When all along, he's been waiting there, waiting to fill us with renewed energy and hope, waiting to remind us of our purpose and equip us to fulfill it, waiting to take our cares upon himself, and waiting to give us the answers we're so desperately seeking everywhere else, but him. And we think, *Where's God?* Well, the real question is, "Where are you?" When are you going to go visit your Father?

> You neglected the Rock who had fathered you;
> you forgot the God who had given you birth.
> (Deuteronomy 32:18)

We put it off, *I'll read the Bible later. I'll pray about that later.* Why later? What's so special about later? Do we think we'll have more time later? Will our schedules free up later? Will we have more energy later, when we get older? I doubt it. And think of all the blessings we miss out on while we wait for later.

It's kind of like when we don't take the opportunity to visit loved ones while we still have them. Or even if we do spend time with our loved ones, we often look back and wish we would have spent even more time because we realize (unfortunately, more so, after they're gone) that we were the ones being blessed by our time together, not just them.

I was really close with my mom. When I was little, she would call me her "shadow" because she couldn't go anywhere without me! Even once I grew up, I always visited her and never stopped relying on her faith and prayers. I loved her so very much. When she became sick, I was there even more and helped to take care of her in her last days, months. But still, what I wouldn't give to get to go back and do more. I thought I was helping her, blessing her, but I realize now that I received way more from her than I ever gave.

My heart breaks to think of the times I complained (maybe not to her, but in my own mind) and actually felt sorry for myself during that time. Seriously, how stupid I feel now, to think that I would indulge myself in any amount of self-pity when she was suffering so. I miss my mom. I was there for her, but I didn't realize that I was the one being blessed by being there. And I had no idea how quickly I would beg for one more day once it was too late.

I Had No Idea

I had no idea it was...
The last time I talked to you on the phone,
The last time I'd feel like your house was home,
The last time I sat with you on your couch,
The last time, over your pillow, you'd slouch,
The last time I brought you groceries from the store,
The last time I'd think, *We can't do this no more.*
The last time I made you something to eat,
The last time I rubbed your swollen feet,
The last time I washed your sink full of dishes,
The last time my heart held onto its wishes,
The last time I brought you your toothbrush and bowl,
The last time I begged God to free your soul...

Until it was...
The first time I couldn't call and hear you say, "Hi,"
The first time I passed your house and just drove on by,
The first time I saw your seat empty and bare,
The first time I saw your pillow just lying there,
The first time I went shopping and didn't take out your list,
The first time I realized those chores would be missed,
The first time in your kitchen, no food to make,
The first time I saw your lotion, but no feet to ache,
The first time no dishes were left in your sink,
The first time I was saddened by the color pink,
The first time I didn't get your toothbrush from its drawer,
The first time I begged God, *Just please, one day more.*

You see, eventually *later* will turn into *too late.* Time keeps on going and runs out—here on earth anyway. So spend time with your loved ones now, including God! No, he's not going to go away, but time does. Opportunities do. People do. You will.

Yes, set aside a special part of the day to read the Bible and pray, but don't limit your time in God's presence to just that time of devotion. Remember you're the one being blessed the most from your time together! So why limit it?

Pray your way through your day! It's gotten to be such a beautiful dependence for me. I don't even want to try making my way through one day without talking to God about everything. As the day unfolds, I ask God for help. I tell him how I feel, what I'm worried about, or what I'm dreading. I ask him questions, I ask him for wisdom, I thank him when good things happen, and I cry out to him when things go wrong. I just talk to him. I couldn't get through a single day without him, and I don't ever want to try!

> Rejoice always, pray without ceasing, give thanks in all circumstances; for this is the will of God in Christ Jesus for you. (1 Thessalonians 5:16–18, ESV)

> Be anxious for nothing, but in everything by prayer and supplication, with thanksgiving, let your requests be made known to God; and the peace of God, which surpasses all understanding, will guard your hearts and minds through Christ Jesus. (Philippians 4:6–8, NKJV)

Just What I Never Knew I Wanted

Do you remember life before the Internet? Life before online shopping? I can. I can remember when I was really little (we're talking late 1970s and early 1980s) when the Sears catalogue would come in the mail. It would be delivered right before Christmas. As soon as I saw it, I would grab it, run into the living room, and plop myself on the couch with catalogue and pen in hand! I would flip to the very back, to the only section that mattered—*the toy section!*

You see, my mom would let me and my sister circle all the toys we liked—no guarantee Santa would bring them; but if we circled them, he would at least know what we wanted. So we would circle away and come Christmas morning, we always got things, not all the things, but at least some of the things we had circled.

Too bad life's not like that. We don't get to flip through a catalogue and circle what we want. We don't get to skip through the sections we don't like and head straight for the "toys." Nope. We get it all. Our Father in heaven knows what we would circle if we had a giant pen, and sometimes, he graciously gives us those things. Other things, he knows we'd never circle, but we wake up one morning and find them "under the tree" anyway.

Consider a time—I'm sure it won't be too hard to think of one—when things didn't work out the way you thought they would, when what you hoped for just didn't happen. Or can you remember a gift you got that was something you would have never, in a million years, wanted? Even with the people closest to us, those who know us best, we can manage to fake it. We plaster a smile on our face, but our heart sinks. Sometimes what we get is not at all what we had hoped for or expected, but it's what we got. And it's still a gift.

Obviously, when your Father in heaven "blesses" you with something and it's not something you wanted, you can't fake a grateful response with him. He knows you too well. But if he knows you that well, then why didn't he get it right? He did.

Now you might think, *God, I didn't circle this! This was not on my list!* But maybe it was on his. Remember, "He knows the plans he has for you" (Jeremiah 29:11, NLT). I wish, and I'm sure you do too, that he would share the details of that plan with us. I wish I could see the big picture like he does. But then again, I probably couldn't take it all in even if he did show me. I don't think I could handle it—right here, right now.

Thank God that in his wisdom, he knows this and only gives me what I can handle *today*. He gives just a little at a time and then provides his guidance each step along the way. "Your word is a lamp unto my feet, and a light unto my path" (Psalm 119:105, NKJV). He doesn't shine a megaflashlight at our feet or on our path, just a little lamp, just enough light to trust him for the next step.

I had a dream a few years back that I was walking up a mountain, and someone was leading me, kind of like a tour guide. (I don't know if he was an angel, but I think he was, that's what makes sense as I look back on it.) Anyway, in my life at that time, I was really confused about some things, and I didn't understand why they were working out the way they were. Whatever God was giving me was definitely "not on my list." I hadn't asked for it, and I didn't want it. In my dream, the tour guide was taking me around this mountain, except we were on the inside of it, climbing up a kind of spiral staircase. As we traveled upward, there were huge pictures (like big-screen TVs) all along the walls.

As I passed each screen, the guide would point out and explain things to me and literally show me "the big picture." How I wish I had that tour guide with me now! Or at least, if I could just remember what he showed me or said to me, but I don't. All I remember was my response to him, "Oh, okay." And then I woke up.

That's it? "Oh, okay." What does that mean? What was I saying,
"Oh, okay," to? The truth is, it doesn't matter. Once I saw the big picture, I understood and accepted it. "Oh, okay"—two simple words,
but if we can muster up the strength and the faith to say these two little words to God, I believe we will find the courage to move forward.

Yeah, it'd be great if he showed us the big picture first. But
chances are, he won't. Consider your faith though, if you can say,
"Oh, okay," now, before seeing the big picture. Could you believe,
without seeing, that the Lord has good intentions for you and that
he will use everything for your good? Could you accept the things
that have happened in your life before understanding them? Could
you submit to God's will before knowing why? Could you trust God
enough to believe that he allows these things for a purpose that's bigger than you, and that he will work out *all things* for your good? Oh,
what great faith that would take! God, give me that faith so that I can
simply say, "Oh, okay," even now.

> Then Jesus told him, "Because you have seen me,
> you have believed; blessed are those who have not
> seen and yet have believed." (John 20:29, NIV)

> And we know that in all things God works
> for the good of those who love him, who have
> been called according to his purpose. (Romans
> 8:28, NIV)

> And without faith it is impossible to please God,
> because anyone who comes to him must believe
> that he exists and that he rewards those who ear-
> nestly seek him. (Hebrews 11:6, NIV)

Settle on that for a second. When we have faith, we please
God. We make our Father proud. Have you ever thought about that
before? That you could actually bring a smile to the face of God?
That's what your faith does!

I would guess, then, that when we don't show any faith, we disappoint or grieve him. When we are at a loss, with no "tour guide" or "big picture" in sight, and we're devastated and find ourselves doubting God, our hearts aren't the only ones breaking. I think it breaks God's heart, too, to see us like that. I think it actually hurts him to hear us questioning his compassion, his listening skills, his ultimate wisdom, and his love for us.

Again, if you are blessed to have a dad like mine, then you know his heart breaks when he watches yours break. He hates seeing you cry. He watches in anguish as you feel like you're being denied answers or withheld love. Well, remember God is your loving heavenly Father, and his heart is ever for you, and breaks for you, and will do anything to protect you.

If you are a parent, then you can also relate. When you watch your child's face fall in disappointment, oh, how your own heart breaks! You long to comfort them and lift their fallen hopes, their downcast face. You'd give anything, do anything, but not at their expense. You're the parent and you know what's best. Your wisdom and protective nature cannot, and should not, cave into their limited understanding and perspective.

And so at times, you may have to withhold from them the very thing they're begging you for because you know it wouldn't be good for them. You can foresee something they can't, and what they want would not be for their ultimate good, so you say no. Even if they cry, even if you cry, you love them too much to give into them. You love them too much to give them what they "circled," and instead, you give them what they need.

They'll thank you later. And later, we'll thank God too.

April Showers Bring May Flowers

But for you who fear my name, the Sun of Righteousness will rise with healing in his wings. And you will go free leaping with joy like calves let out to pasture.
—Malachi 4:2 (NLT)

Spring is finally here—at least the rain is. I woke up this morning and looked out the window, wet and gray. That's all right. For the first time in a long time, I felt sunshine in my heart, like a hopeful little dandelion inside me, one of those fluffy white ones, waiting for the wind to blow just right and make its wish come true.

I didn't wake up this way, but I stayed in bed a little longer, prayed a little more, read my Bible a little bit, and just allowed the Holy Spirit to bring me some peace. There is healing in his wings, and heaven knows I need it. My heart still feels shattered into a billion pieces, but somehow after spending some quiet time with my Father this morning, I feel hopeful and grateful. Grateful for the rain. I thought about it. Rain is a gift from God. The heavens open up and down it pours on us. It may not look pretty or feel warm. It may very well ruin our plans. But without it, nothing grows.

If rain is the gift, then flowers are the gratitude. The thankful stretch back to heaven from where all blessings flow. Flowers know enough to reach up as far as they can and thank God. They are grateful for all that he provides: the sun, the rain, the wind—all that's necessary for life and growth. They're thankful for all that it took to make them push through the dirt, through all the hard ground, and maybe even a little "fertilizer," to see the direction in which they were pointed all along, and to finally bloom into the beautiful creation God made them to be... even if that's just a little dandelion.

Turn It Off

A while back, I was driving along with my son in the back seat of our truck. I don't remember where we were going, but I remember the song that came on the radio. "Mom! That song makes you sad. Turn it off!"

My little boy (he was very young at the time) felt my pain from the back seat and wanted me to turn it off. I'm not sure if he got a glimpse of my face in the rearview mirror, and maybe my sunglasses were not big enough to hide the tears behind them, I don't know, but he read my expression like the words on this page. He could feel my heart sinking as soon as the song started—drowning. And he was right. That song flooded my mind with memories I wish I could wipe out forever, but I can't.

"I can't turn it off," I told him. "Everything makes me sad." I knew I shouldn't have said that, not to my son, but it was the truth, and it just spilled out.[2] And then so did the tears. The truth was that if I turned off every song that made me sad, I'd never listen to another song. I'd never look out the window to see my favorite kind

---

[2] A little disclaimer: In case you're wondering, I did correct my actions with my son. I knew I shouldn't have said, "Everything makes me sad." Like I said, it just spilled out. It wasn't my finest hour. Anyway, I told him, almost immediately, that I was sorry and I shouldn't have said what I said. I explained that although there were many things that made me feel sad at that time, because of what we were going through, there were also many things that made me feel happy, especially him! I was also able to use this to teach him that we all feel sad sometimes, that's just part of life, but when we do, we get to go to God in prayer and ask him to help us work through it. Thank God we can go back and apologize to our kids, and that they are so quick to forgive our imperfections. I feel that as long as we're honest with them and humble enough to admit when we're wrong, then they will love and learn from us all the more. Thank God.

of morning with one of those beautiful pink sunrises. I'd never sit around another crackling fire, or roast marshmallows, or watch the sunset, or go fishing, or go for a long drive, or just out for ice cream. I'd never...

The list just goes on. It never ends and neither does the pain, so I can't turn it off. I'd be living blindly in a silent world. And even then my heart would remember.

The thing is, I'm not willing to shut out all the beauty of this life, this world. What my Father created is far too wonderful to deprive myself of; and so I just have to continue to invite his healing love into my heart, into my wounds, and trust him that it will get easier and less painful—someday.

A friend of mine once told me that when she was going through a devastating time in her life, what kept her hanging on was one thought. "I can't give up," she would tell herself, "because my miracle is coming, and it might come tomorrow."

If that's all you've got—hope for tomorrow—then that's enough. Hang onto it, you're entitled to it! As a child of God, you are entitled to enjoy the sound of his birds waking you up in the morning, and the beauty of a golden wheat field, and the sparkling of his stars in the night sky. I won't close my eyes to his works, or my ears to his words, and you shouldn't either. Wait on the Lord and for his joy to fill your heart again; and in the meantime, keep on living.

> I would have lost heart, unless I had believed
> That I would see the goodness of the Lord
> In the land of the living.
> Wait on the Lord;
> Be of good courage,
> And He shall strengthen your heart;
> Wait, I say on the Lord! (Psalm 27:13–14, NKJV)

> And hope does not disappoint us, because God
> has poured out his love into our hearts by the Holy
> Spirit, whom he has given us. (Romans 5:5 NKJV)

Unfinished Poem

I would have been better off
to have never known,
to have been a flower,
that had never grown.

Yeah, whoever said,
"Better to have loved and lost..."
They never loved.
Never knew the cost...

The above is a poem I started, but never finished. I just kind of gave up on it. Fitting. I'm sure you can relate. Somethings, you just can't finish. Sometimes, you're just too tired, you need a break, you give up. You've just got to put down whatever it is you're carrying. I want to tell you, it's okay to put it down.

You were never meant to carry everything. You don't have to finish everything you start. Life is not an endurance contest. In the end, no one receives an award for "The Most Stressed," or "Juggled the Most," or "Carried Their Burdens the Longest." These are not goals, and they're certainly not rewards—they're just unhealthy demands.

They're demands we put on ourselves and burdens put on us by others. They weren't meant for you to carry forever—your shoulders just aren't that big. But you know whose are? "Then Jesus said,

'Come to me, all of you who are weary and carry heavy burdens, and I will give you rest'" (Matthew 11:28, NLT).

Dear God,

I'm coming to you for rest. Jesus promised it to me. I need it. What happened? How could this be my life? It's nothing like I imagined it would be when I was little. I just don't get it, and I want to give up. I'm tired of trying to figure it all out. I'm done trying to make sense of this pain, as if somehow that would make it more bearable, worthwhile even. I trust you that all of it was for a reason; make me okay with not knowing what that reason is, for now. I'm sick of rethinking and retracing history like I do, trying to understand everything. I can't understand; I can't right every wrong, and I'm tired of trying. I can't make sense of it, Lord.

Love,
Me

The following thoughts came to me while I was praying, and even though they seem kind of vague, they're enough for now.

1.   It doesn't make sense because it doesn't make sense.
2.   You can go crazy trying to figure out something that's crazy.

What does that mean? Well, I think it means that it's a futile endeavor to attempt to rationalize the irrational. You're not going to do it. You'll go crazy trying. You can't make the insensible make sense. You can't resolve the unresolvable. I'm not saying God can't. But you can't, and you'll lose it if you try.

The human mind can't handle it; you've just got to give it to God. Give it up, let it go. If it made sense, if it was right, you'd have figured it out by now. It doesn't fit into your mind frame and ideals because it shouldn't! Crazy things will happen in this life, and if you can't make sense of it, good. You don't want to! Some things should never make sense or seem right because they're not.

Ugh, how I've labored in vain to figure out and resolve things that were just screwed up to begin with!

The fact that we are bothered, frustrated, or even shocked by some things only illustrates what we are up against. In this world, we daily face untruth and confusion, and we can't straighten it out in our minds because it's crooked! Don't call a crooked line straight. Don't call wrong right. Some things are just wrong, and you feel dismayed because you are right! This world, in all its sin and confusion, will try to make you feel like you're wrong because it doesn't make sense to you, when the truth is, it just doesn't make sense.

I mean, God's Word warns us about what the world is going to be like, and you don't have to look far to see his truth unfolding. Read the following passage from 2 Timothy:

> Be sure of this. In the last days hard times will come. People will love themselves. They will love money. They will talk about themselves and be proud. They will say wrong things about people. They will not obey their parents. They will not be thankful. They will not keep anything holy. They will have no love. They will not agree with anybody. They will tell lies about people. They will have no self-control. They will beat people. They will not love anything that is good. They cannot be trusted. They will act quickly, without thinking. They are proud of themselves. They love to have fun more than they love God. They act as if they worshipped God, yet they do not let God's power work in their lives... And they want to do many kinds of wrong things. They are always trying to learn, but never able to find out what is really true. (2 Timothy 3:1–7, WE)

Sound familiar? It does to me. This *is* the world we live in. Don't try to figure it out—just recognize it's messed up and needs Jesus! It's not right, and we can't pretend it is. Don't try to rationalize or justify it; its behaviors are not rational and cannot be justified. If we try to understand it, become sympathetic to it, or worse yet make excuses for it, we'll be deceived by it.

I don't know about you, but I don't want to understand a world like that, and I certainly don't want to fit into it. I don't want to be okay in a world in which right is wrong and wrong is right. I should be baffled by that, and I am. This world doesn't make sense to me; it's not supposed to. It's not my home.

I pray that those who are content with the wrong in this world will grow discontent. I pray that their eyes would be opened to the truth and that they would no longer feel pride in their wayward lives. I pray that God would humble their hearts and that they would cry out in repentance. My hope is that they would realize that God had a better way, still has a better way, for them to live their lives, and it's still possible! I beg God, before it's too late, to show them that although they thought they were right, they were wrong. And I pray that they will cry out to God as I have.

My Right Was So Wrong!

I've been so right, I was wrong
And so wrong, I was right.
I've been wound up
Bound up
Bitter and tight.
I've judged you
And I've smudged you
But mostly...
I loved you.
Believe me when I tell you,
I just wanted to belong;
And I'm sorry,
So sorry...
My right was so wrong.

Dear Father,

Give us humble, repentant hearts. Give us wisdom to discern right from wrong, and your Holy Spirit to shed light on our decisions. We ask for forgiveness for all those times we thought we were right, but weren't. And we ask for your guidance and grace to think the right thoughts, say the right words, make the right choices, and live life the right way. Because despite what the world says, there is still a right way and a wrong way. Don't let us be deceived. We live in a world of relativism, but there are still absolutes. And God, you are that Absolute. You are the authority and final judge of what is right and wrong. You are the Absolute Truth—the one who never changes. Thank you for being that solid rock on which we stand, the one we can count on when all other rocks crumble and fall. Thank you for being *God*.

Love,
Me

There is a way that seems right to a man, but in the end is the way of death. (Proverbs 14:12, NKJV)

Lord, keep us and our children from this way, which seems right but in the end leads to death. Humble us and teach us to follow only you, and lead us in your everlasting way.

Search me, O God, and know my heart: try me, and know my thoughts: And see if there be any wicked way in me and lead me in the way everlasting. (Psalm 139:23–24, KJV)

Fill in the Blank

"You wanted to give yourself to _____. I wanted you to give yourself to me. It's not the same thing." Go ahead, fill in the blank yourself. This is just something I feel God spoke to my heart, and it really made me think. I know what I was filling in that blank with, and it wasn't God. What would you write in that blank? What (or who) have you been trying to give your all to? How's that going? If it's not God, then my guess is it's not going well. You're probably feeling frustrated, unsatisfied, and lonely. Now, we know there are so many valuable, even honorable, options to choose from, things to fill that blank in with; in fact, if this were a multiple-choice question (usually easier to answer than fill-in-the-blank questions), it might read as follows:

I wanted to give myself to:

A. my job
B. my spouse
C. my children
D. my hobbies
E. all of the above

Look, even if all your options are *good*, it's not the same as *God*. In fact, where is he on that list? Even if you choose "all of the above," you wouldn't get it right. You wouldn't pass the test.

Notice the statement is deliberately in past tense because if you're honestly asking yourself this, whoever/whatever you devoted yourself to (if not God) has already failed you. Or rather, you failed—you chose the wrong answer. But thank God for retakes and makeup tests. Life is a series of do-overs, and we can always reassess ourselves and make changes and corrections. We haven't taken the final exam yet, so there's still time to pass! And until we do, God will keep giving us chances to make a better choice. He is a merciful teacher. He might even give you the same test over and over until you pass. You see, he doesn't want you to fail.

I am a middle-school teacher, and at my school, we offer kids the option to retake any quiz that they may have done poorly on before taking the final test. My middle schoolers are great at taking advantage of this option. They don't feel bad about asking for a retake. Why do we though, as adults, feel so ashamed admitting that we screwed up or even just that we weren't prepared, and want to try again? We teach our kids to learn from their mistakes and to try again, as many times as it takes, to get it right. So why do we beat ourselves up so badly when we need a do-over? And why is it so hard to see God as a merciful, patient teacher who will do everything he can to make sure that we learn our lessons and succeed in life? He wants us all to get A's. He doesn't want one of us to fail. "The Lord isn't really being slow about his promise, as some people think. No, he is being patient for your sake. He does not want anyone to be destroyed but wants everyone to repent" (2 Peter 3:9, NLT).

He wants everyone to learn from their mistakes and move on to the abundant life he promised. He is the most patient teacher you have ever had or will ever have. He is not going to take out his red pen and mark giant X's all over your life. His Son already took all the marks for our mistakes. So don't be afraid—go ahead and repent of your sins and ask for another chance. He won't deny you. If only we could remember that—that he's got us. He's the only one with the right answer. He is the answer. He's the only secure place we can rest, and if we are choosing him, or filling our blanks with him, then we really can have that "peace...which surpasses all understanding" (Philippians 4:7, ESV). When we're in his hands, we can rest our heads and our hearts. "See, I have engraved you on the palms of my hands; your walls are ever before me" (Isaiah 49:16, NIV).

I know it may seem like I'm repeating myself all throughout this book, but remember this is my journaling. My thought process. My lessons. And God knows I need my lessons repeated. We all learn from repetition or need repetition to learn (some of us more than others). But the more I think about this, the more times I have to repeat my lessons, the more I realize that *he* is the answer.

I keep relearning the importance of *only* resting in him. We cannot make anyone else the one on whom we rest our weary heads and heavy hearts. When we find our security in someone or something else, or even in ourselves, then that actually becomes our god. And any other god will ultimately turn you inward because it will not love and fulfill you like God would. So you'll be looking inward all the time, trying to fill the voids (all the blanks) in your own life. Therefore, a cycle of wrong worship begins.

The thing you worship (spend all your time, energy, and focus on) will leave you empty. So then in order to fill your emptiness (because "it" can't), you will become consumed with trying to fill it yourself. You'll start to focus on you, obsess on your own needs/wants, and begin putting all your energy into self-improvement. You'll continually invest in yourself. The result will be selfishness.

You will try to make yourself more whatever (more beautiful, more successful, smarter, skinnier, funnier, more energetic, more independent, more confident, more accepted, more loved…more whatever) in order to be able to get a return on your investment. But it will never come.

You won't realize that you're being selfish; in fact, you may feel quite the opposite. You'll feel neglected, you'll feel like the victim, and you'll feel justified in your self-consumption because you'll think, *I have to take care of myself, no one else will.* But in reality, you were worshiping the wrong thing in the first place; it failed you, and now you're trying to meet your own needs when only God can.

I think that's why so many people (myself included, at times) become so self-centered. It's an easy pit to fall into. It's not conceit; it's the opposite, really. You may even despise yourself, and you just want to be better, more whatever. You just want to be happy, you just want to be loved. You're searching for fulfillment or whatever it is you're so desperately trying to feel. But you won't find it because you're not looking in the right place.

It's called idolatry.

You may be thinking, *What? I don't worship idols!* God said, "You shall have no other gods before me" (Exodus 20:3, NIV). The thing is, he wasn't just talking about statues and shrines. I remember reading the Bible and so many times thinking, *Why would anyone be so stupid as to worship a statue? No wonder God would get so mad at them!* I had no idea what it really meant, or how it's still a relevant command today and in our own lives.

When I thought of idolatry, I imagined the golden calf or some other image of a fake god and people actually kneeling before it. I thought of ancient civilizations bowing, and even sacrificing to a manmade idol. I didn't realize that a manmade idol is anything we make or set up for ourselves that becomes our Number One.

When God said that we "shall have no other gods before" him, he meant *anything*—even ourselves. You may not think you put yourself before God, but be honest, who do you think of more? Who do you try to satisfy? Who do you expect to come through for you? Who are you relying on?

We have been taught in our society to be independent and self-sufficient. I have to admit, when I was a single mom, I prided myself in the fact that I could take care of myself and my son. I know that's not accurate. I know we'd have had nothing if it weren't for God providing it, but much of my self-esteem came from that wrong mind-set. How foolish! I need God, my Father, for every breath I take! I'm nothing without him and can do nothing apart from him!

> But they are deeply guilty, for their own strength is their god. (Habakkuk 1:11, NLT)

> How foolish to trust in your own creation. (Habakkuk 2:18, NLT)

Idolatry is a continual inward and downward spiral. You take your eyes off God and put them on something that will inevitably fail you and destroy you, even if it *is* you! You'll become an empty vessel, trying to fill itself. And it'll never happen. You'll never be fulfilled until you put your eyes back on God. Serve and worship him—the only real source of everything your heart desires.

> Take delight in the Lord, and he will give you the desires of your heart. (Psalm 37:4 NIV)

Thank you, Jesus, for clean pages, new notebooks, and endless chances to start over. Thank you that we don't have to remain empty vessels. Thank you for not only fixing, but filling our broken, empty hearts like only you can! It reminds me of your first miracle in the Bible. The vessels of wine were empty, and it was a wedding. I think you love love—after all, you created it! Perhaps you're the biggest romantic there is! You knew how special the wedding was and how important every detail was to the bride and groom, and you took those empty vessels and filled them. It's just like us, we spill, get used up, dried out, cracked, and emptied; and then you come along, like an unexpected guest, and do something miraculous, something only you could do; you fill us back up again. You take our nothingness and turn it into something wonderful!

> You have turned for me my mourning into dancing. (Psalm 30:11, ESV)

The Bible refers to us as "jars of clay." Lord, you know clay jars are hard, they're breakable, fragile, and exhaustible. But you—you fix us, put us back together again (even stronger than before we broke), and then fill us with "new wine," new life, and new love.

> Behold, I make all things new. (Revelations 2:15, KJV)

The Authority to Comfort

We know that God deserves the place of honor and worship in our hearts and in our lives. He is the only fount from which all blessings flow. He is the only one who can heal, restore, and fill our lives. He is the only one with the authority to judge, deliver, free, save, heal, forgive, and comfort.

> The Spirit of the Sovereign Lord is upon me,
> for the Lord has anointed me
> to bring good news to the poor.
> He has sent me to comfort the brokenhearted
> and to proclaim that captives will be released
> and prisoners will be freed.
> He has sent me to tell those who mourn
> that the time of the Lord's favor has come,
> and with it, the day of God's anger against their enemies.
> To all who mourn in Israel,
> he will give a crown of beauty for ashes,
> a joyous blessing instead of mourning,
> festive praise instead of despair. (Isaiah 61:1–3, NLT)

Please, Father,

Comfort me. You're the only one who has the authority. Anything someone else might say to comfort me may or may not be true. I can't rest in anyone else's words. Even if they think they're comforting me with truthful words, they don't know. No one else feels my past, understands my present, or can see my future, so how could I trust them to be right? How could I put confidence in their words like I can in yours? You tell us in Psalm 138 that your promises are backed by all the honor of your name—that's why and how I can believe what you say. Every word. The Bible also says that the earth will shake at the force of your Word. Father, I don't take your words lightly. I believe them. I cling to them. Without them, there is no real comfort or hope.

I've had friends, family, and even "strong Christians" try to comfort and advise me; but sometimes, their guess is as good (or as bad) as mine. And many times, I'm sorry I listened to them. But you, oh God, you know the beginning from the end. When you say something, the earth shakes! When you declare a word, nothing can stop it. Therefore, I choose to listen to you and only you. Lord, I only want to hear your voice. Let it pour into me and over me. Speak into my heart. Shine your light into the darkness of my sorrow. Give me, even one word, to hang onto.

Love,
Me

GPS

I am once again amazed how God can take simple everyday experiences and through them teach heavenly principles. My church was participating in a community prayer meeting, and I had been thinking about attending, but as usual was hindered by my fear of driving anywhere unknown. If this meeting were to be held right at my church, there would have been no doubt I would go. However, this meeting was to be in held in a different city (mind you, not even that far from my own, but I am such a chicken when it comes to driving anywhere outside of my little comfort zone). I realize that my fear of getting lost may be somewhat irrational, but it is nonetheless real, and it has kept me from going many places that I would have otherwise loved to have gone. So I almost did not attend this event. Just the thought of going out, by myself, at night to a place I was unsure of made me want to avoid the whole thing. I could just hear about it later from everyone else and find out how it went.

Then I thought, *Wait a minute, I have a GPS now!* Keep in mind this was a time when GPS was a fairly new luxury, for me anyway. Doubting even my skills to be able to use the GPS properly, I still asked a couple of people if they were going first or if they wanted to go, that way I wouldn't have to rely on myself, and even if we got lost, we would at least be lost together (not nearly as scary).

But everyone I knew, well enough to ask, was not planning on going. I debated back and forth in my mind; I was getting so frustrated with myself because I knew that to any normal person, this would be nothing—no big deal at all. But for me, it was this huge dilemma, it always was when it came to this kind of a thing, and I was sick of it. I prayed again, "God, what should I do?" The word "Go!" came to me as plainly as anything. *Okay*, I thought, *I'm going.*

I put the address in my GPS and headed out. Even though I was nervous, I felt really good that I was pushing past this fear that had always held me back. I was trusting God; he told me to go, and I was obeying. (And I was learning how to use my GPS.)

I made it there and on time! Only to be disappointed. The overall message was *nice* but not *powerful*. The music didn't move me either. I looked around...no one I really knew that well, mostly strangers. Ugh. I felt so alone. I drove all the way there alone, sat there alone, and didn't feel anything but *alone*. Why did God tell me to go?

Then the thought came to me, *Maybe the lesson I needed to learn tonight was not going to be preached by the pastor. Maybe it wasn't something I was going to get from "being" in church, but rather in "going" to church.* It was about stepping out in faith. The journey, not the destination. I knew I didn't know the way, I knew I'd get lost if I tried to get there on my own abilities, but God was leading me, so I went.

Not sure of how to get there, but determined to get there, I relied on my GPS. Suddenly it hit me—God's Pathfinding System. Analogies started to flood my mind as I sat there in that meeting, no longer paying attention to anything they were saying, but just being amazed at the new revelation God was giving me in that moment.

For example, I didn't follow my GPS perfectly. The path was laid out perfectly, but I took a couple of wrong turns. I also avoided the expressway that my GPS told me to take, and that would have gotten me there a lot quicker, but I took the longer route because of my own fears.

But I still got there. Every time I missed the mark, missed the turn, or went my own way, it *recalculated!* It took into account my errors and simply brought me to the next road that would lead me to my destination.

Isn't that just like God? He lays out the perfect plan, knowing full well we won't take it. He knows we'll mess up. He knows we'll think our way is better, and we'll take that. He waits. Knowing that our way will only delay our arrival and waste our energy, he waits. He's a patient Father. And if we look to him, he will get us there, eventually, despite our mistakes. God tells us that his grace will even make our mistakes to prosper (Psalm 1:3).

He takes into account our weaknesses, our mistakes, and all our wrong turns. He recalculates our wanderings and provides us with a new route to get back on the right path—the one that will, in the end, lead us to our destination. We will, no matter how bad we mess up, get there if we will just put our eyes back on him, on our spiritual GPS, and keep on truckin'.

But if you want God to lead you, you have to plug into his "system." If you don't, you *will* get lost. If you keep trying to go your own way, you won't get there. The path you end up on (apart from him) will not lead you to your ultimate destination because he is the only way. Jesus tells us, "I am the way and the truth and the life. No one comes to the Father except through me" (John 14:6, NIV).

How often do we insist on doing things our own way, wind up lost, and actually get mad at God! I can tell you it's not God who gets us lost. We'll never head in the wrong direction *if* we're following his directions (commands and instructions in the Bible, as well as the promptings of the Holy Spirit). What gets us lost is sin, selfishness, pride, feeling sorry for ourselves—the list goes on and on. There are so many wrong roads to take, so many dead-end turns to make.

Dead-End Turnin'

Always yearnin'
Not quite right,
Candle's burnin'
All through the night.

But I still can't see
Where I went wrong...
And I can't remember the words
To my favorite song

No more.

Why do I do
All this hard-way learnin'
Why do I do
So much dead-end turnin'?

I swear each time,
It won't be the same
But I know it's me...
Won't pass no blame

No more.

God save me from
This road I'm drivin'
Save me from
All this empty strivin.'

In your mercy
Light my way,
Crank up
That song
And let it play...

Till maybe I remember the words

Again

Someday.

As an English teacher, I actually cringed as I wrote this poem, the poor grammar and all the double negatives. But it kind of just fit, and it made me think about all the "double negatives" we make in our lives when we set our own course. We realize that we've made a mistake, took a wrong turn on our journey, and we want to correct it. Here's the key—without true repentance, correction won't work, and it won't last. You'll just take another wrong turn and then another, trying to undo the damage from the first mistake, but by then you've meandered about all over the place, making wrong turn after wrong turn until you're completely lost and can't even remember where you started.

Did your mom ever tell you, "Two wrongs don't make a right?" My mom did; I heard that a lot. Turns out, Mom knew what she was talking about (always did). You see, if you make a wrong turn (choice) and rather than repenting and turning away from it, you just make another wrong turn (choice) trying to get out of the first one… that still won't make you right or get you going in the right direction. You won't be right until you make it right with God. You won't be right until you repent (ask God for forgiveness) and turn your heart and your whole self away from that sin. You can't stay in it and get anywhere, at least not anywhere good. You can change directions a million times, spend your whole life doing that, but unless you're following God, you'll still be lost.

Listen, we can't blame God when we make a wrong turn! We can't get mad at him when our lives feel hopeless and we feel lost and all alone. The truth is we have to take the responsibility of "plugging in" to his Word, his wisdom, and rely on him to get us back on the right path and moving forward. We are never alone, he's always there, waiting, and we don't have to be lost for long.

If you feel you have gotten sidetracked and now you're lost, tell him you want his guidance *and determine yourself to follow it!* Maybe you know exactly where you took that wrong turn, maybe you haven't got a clue; either way, call out to him. You might be more than just a little sidetracked; you might be going completely in the opposite direction of where your destination (or destiny) lies. The road you're on right now may not lead to anywhere you'd ever want to go, so you desperately need God's help, and you need it in a hurry! Don't wander any further before asking for it. Stop what you're doing, right now, and call out to your Father, "I'm lost, help me!" He will. He'll go to great lengths to save you. Even if he has to completely turn you around and recalculate your whole life, he can and he will, but you have to listen. You have to choose his way, not your own.

Now this may not happen overnight. How many miles have you wandered? How many years have you been lost? Well, it might take some time getting you back on track, but you have to be patient too, obedient to his leading, and persistent in fixing your eyes on him as you go.

> So be careful to do what the Lord your God has commanded you; do not turn aside to the right or the left. Walk in obedience to all that the Lord your God has commanded you, so that you may live and prosper and prolong your days in the land that you will possess. (Deuteronomy 5:32–33, NIV)

That night at church continued to open up my eyes to more revelation and a better understanding of this message. I eventually did find some friends that I knew from my own church there. Somewhere in our conversation that evening, I explained how I hadn't been sure of how to get there and how I used my GPS even though the place was not even that far. I was kind of just laughing at myself, but they kindly offered to let me follow them back. They said that if I had taken the expressway, it would have been a lot less complicated, and if I followed them back on it, I'd get home much quicker. Even though I now knew I didn't necessarily *need* to follow anybody, it was a reassuring offer, so I took them up on it. I still put my home address in my GPS, just in case.

We were on the expressway, they were in front of me, and I was trying my best to keep up. When we got to a certain point though, they had to veer off in another direction to get to their destination, while I had to stay in my lane to get to mine. That too illuminated a new truth as brightly as my headlights illuminated the black pavement in front of me—you can't follow anybody else to get to *your* destination. You can talk to people, seek godly counsel, look up to and learn from others, and glean from their wisdom; but no one's path is exactly the same as yours, so you can't follow someone else's GPS. You have to develop a trusting relationship with your Father who wants to guide you, and he is the only one on whom you can completely rely and follow.

When you were little, did your dad ever let you sit on top of his shoulders? As he'd walk around, you'd have what felt like a bird's-eye view. You could see everything from way up there! Maybe you were at a big event, and he didn't want you to get lost in the crowd. Maybe he was demonstrating his strength or maybe just playing around, having some fun with you. Whatever the reason was, from up there, you could see much farther ahead than you ever could have down on your level.

I think it's like that sometimes with God. Sometimes if we're in a dangerous place and we're lost, or he wants to keep us from getting lost, he just lifts us up, high on his shoulders, and carries us to safety. "The eternal God is your refuge, and underneath are the everlasting arms" (Deuteronomy 33:27, NIV).

I know he does this because when I look back on some of my most painful experiences, I wonder, *How in the world did I ever get through that? How did I survive that heartache, or how did I get out of that mess?* Well, I know it was my Father picking me up because I could not have pushed my way through the obstacles and oppression myself. It must have been him, and it was. It was by his power and grace alone. With his strong, everlasting arms, he sets us above our circumstances so that we can see our way again.

Other times, though, he doesn't just pick us up, and we don't get that vantage point or clear view of where we're going. Instead, we have to just trust him even though we can't see the road ahead. We learn to rely on him, just like we rely on our GPS when we're driving along, and it only shows us the next short distance or the next immediate turn. Why is it we can have blind faith and complete confidence in a manmade device (our GPS or phone) but somehow cannot afford God that same trust? He made the man who made the device that we do rely on, yet we don't really believe he—the Creator of the universe and everything in it—is capable of getting us to our destination. It's crazy when you think of it like that!

Besides, part of the reason we lose our way is to teach us to trust God and rely on him alone. So the more we fight it, the more we strive to carve out our own path, the farther we get from home. We all have joked around about those individuals who just won't stop and ask for directions (I'm sure you can think of a few). No matter how lost they get, they are bound and determined to find their own way. They want to go it alone. They don't want help from anyone.

Don't be that person. Ask for directions; seek God and trust him to get you there. Take advice from someone who knows what it's like to always feel lost, someone who has no sense of direction of her own—follow your "GPS."

> Stand at the crossroads and look: ask for the ancient paths, ask where the good way is, and walk in it, and you will find rest for your souls. But you said, "We will not walk in it." (Jeremiah 6:16, NIV)

Again, don't be that person! Don't be the one who says, "No, I will not walk in your way." Please, you're heading for a dark journey and a lost life if you do! God knows how desperately each of us needs for him to direct our hearts and guide our steps. If it weren't so important, it wouldn't have been mentioned so many times throughout the Bible. Take a look at the following references; these are just a few:

> Be very strong; be careful to obey all that is written in the Book of the Law of Moses, without turning to the right or to the left. (Joshua 23:6, NIV)

> I will instruct and teach you in the way you should go; I will counsel you with my loving eye on you. (Psalm 32:8, NIV)

> The Lord makes firm the steps of the one who delights in him. (Psalm 37:23, NIV)

Direct my footsteps according to your word; let no sin rule over me. (Psalm 119:133, NIV)

Blessed are all who fear the Lord, who walk in obedience to him. (Psalm 128:1, NIV)

Let me hear in the morning of your steadfast love, for in you I trust. Make me know the way I should go, for to you I lift up my soul. Deliver me from my enemies, O Lord! I have fled to you for refuge. Teach me to do your will, for you are my God! Let your good Spirit lead me on level ground! (Psalm 143:8–10, ESV)

Trust in the Lord with all thine heart; and lean not unto thine own understanding. In all thy ways acknowledge him, and he shall direct thy paths. (Proverbs 3:5–6, KJV)

Don't get sidetracked; keep your feet from following evil. (Proverbs 4:27, NLT)

When Jesus spoke again to the people, he said, "I am the light of the world. Whoever follows me will never walk in darkness but will have the light of life." (John 8:12, NIV)

Since we live by the Spirit, let us keep in step with the Spirit. (Galatians 5:25, NIV)

May the Lord direct your hearts into God's love and Christ's perseverance. (2 Thessalonians 3:5, NIV)

Trust

My prayer is that one day I will learn to rely on God, my Father, as easily as I relied on my dad when I was little, that is, without even having to think about it. I can remember long rides home with my dad. If he was driving his truck (this is before bucket seats), I could lie down on the horse blanket he had stretched across the whole seat and rest my head on his lap (yes, this was also before seat belt laws). I'd lay down and just fall asleep. I never once worried, *I hope my dad knows where we're going,* or *I hope he knows how to get us home!* Those thoughts never occurred to me, doubt never entered my mind. He knew the way, and I rested. Half the time, I'd wake up as I sensed the garage light coming on when we pulled in, and I'd think, *Oh, wow, we're home already!* I know our Father in heaven longs for us to rest on him like that. Believe me, he knows the way. He is the Way!

Trust is an amazing thing. It can be a one-way thing, or it can be a two-way thing. It kind of just depends. When I was little, it was definitely a one-way thing. I relied completely on my dad; I trusted and depended on him. It wasn't a mutual thing. I was smart to trust him, and he was smart *not* to trust me. Of course he couldn't, not at first anyway. Think about it, when we're little, we have to completely rely on our parents. We trust them, but they can't trust us with anything. But as we grow and mature, they can begin to trust us with a few things. As we continue to grow, they continue to trust us with more and more.

I bring this up because not too long ago, I was driving my dad to one of his doctor appointments. I used to rely on him driving me everywhere, but now he relies on me. Remember how I said I'd often fall asleep while he drove me home? Well, we were in his car (he can't climb up into my big truck, so I have to drive his car when I take him places), and I was talking to him. I can't remember what I was talking about it, but I noticed he had been quiet for quite a while. When I looked over to make sure he could hear me, I saw that he was fast asleep. It made me smile. I thought, *It's your turn to rest and trust me now.*

Even though he's my dad and he will always have my trust, over time, the trust has become reciprocal. Building trust takes time and requires integrity. You have to prove that you can, and will, do the right thing. Over the years, I have proven to my dad that I can, and will, do the right thing; he can trust me. And so he slept, like a baby, in the passenger seat without a care in world, while I sat in the driver's seat and took him where he needed to go. Trust, like love, is best when it's mutual.

I wonder if my Father in heaven can trust me like that. In some areas, maybe. In other areas, not yet. That's okay. Remember building trust takes time. The more we learn (from our mistakes), the more we eventually get it right, the more God can trust us with. It's like the New Testament parable when the master is pleased with his servant's effort and accomplishment. "His master said to him, 'Well done, good and faithful servant! You have been faithful over a little; I will set you over much. Enter into the joy of your master!'" (Matthew 25:21).

I like to think of the trust that grows between two people as a trust bond. That bond is strengthened and the relationship deepens the more we learn that we can rely on each other. That kind of relationship can exist between us and our Master, our heavenly Father, just like it can exist between a parent and a child or in any other type of relationship in which we develop that bond.

Trust. It's a beautiful thing.

Still Waters

He leads me besides still waters, he restores my soul.
—Psalm 23:2–3 (NKJV)

The idea came to me that maybe still waters are our collected tears. We read that the Holy Spirit, our Comforter, bottles our tears. "You have collected all my tears in your bottle" (Psalm 56:8, NLT). And I wonder, when he restores our souls, if the extent of our peace—or still waters—will equate with the amount of tears we've shed. Sometimes the pain we've gone through becomes a blurry memory, not faded or dulled, every bit as painful, but clouded by so many tears that we can't even remember who to blame, how it all happened, why it happened, or even what happened! We just don't know anymore. All we have are these tears. They feel endless and we feel forgotten. But we can be sure, if we trust his Word, that he is collecting them, noticing and remembering each one. He's bottling them up, only to later pour them out as still waters with which to restore our souls. So I thank you, Father, for every tear, every last drop.

When He Reigns, He Pours

You've heard the saying, "When it rains, it pours." That usually has a negative connotation, like when one bad thing happens, a whole bunch of bad things happen. One thing just kind of follows the other. Well, I can think of something else that naturally goes together like that, only this is a very good thing—when he reigns, he pours. When he reigns in your life, when you give him complete authority over everything and submit to him alone, then he will pour out his Spirit and blessings like you've never known before. I know this, I believe this, but when will I actually live like this?

Dear Father,

When will I let you truly reign in my life? Many of us, Christians, say (even brag) of our faith in you. We say things like, "God's in complete control." Really? Do we really let you control everything in our lives? Do we really let you reign supreme over everything—our will, our plans, our conversations, our thoughts? Or do we just give you the territory we don't want to deal with and ask you to set up your kingdom there?

I'm convinced (and ashamed) that that's what we do, at least much of the time. We pray for your will, proclaim your Word over our lives, but give you control only over the areas that we *want* to see your hand in. But other areas, we hold onto or even try to hide from you. I think that if we're honest with ourselves, and with you,

God, then we'd admit there are some decisions we don't invite you into. There are some problems we don't want fixed the way we think you'd fix them. There are some battles we insist on fighting our own way. There may even be some temptations we don't want to be led away from. So we don't let you reign—and so you cannot pour.

The reason I believe this is because I see what our lives look like. If you were really reigning in our lives, then we'd be experiencing a whole lot more pouring of your Spirit. We'd see more of your blessings, favor, healing…just more of *you* in our everyday lives, if only we'd let you into our everyday lives, all of it.

Therefore, if we want more of you—your love, compassion, forgiveness, grace, strength, peace, and power—to pour into our lives and through our lives, then we must submit to your sovereignty and let you reign. We need to get down on our knees, bow to your authority, and humble ourselves to your will in *every* area.

Father, you gave us free will; therefore, we need to *choose* to give you control in our lives and to let you reign in them. You'll never force your rule in our hearts, you'll wait to be invited. You're not a dictator. You are a righteous, gracious King. The more we submit to you, the more you'll reign, and the more you reign, the more you'll pour.

Love,
Me

Without a Vision

Dear Father,

I know that the dreams you place in the hearts of your children are attainable. You give us a vision, and if we rely on you and pursue you, you bring us to it. You complete what you started and make what was once only a vision a reality. I know we'd be hopeless without the vision, whatever it may be, that you've placed in our hearts.

"Where there is no vision, the people perish" (Proverbs 29:18, KJV).

I don't doubt your power to make my dreams come true, as cliché as that may sound. My problem is not knowing what to dream. I don't doubt you, but I do doubt me. I've fallen short of my hopes and dreams so many times that I doubt my ability to know what (or even how) to dream anymore.

Could I have possibly moved so far away from my center, in you, that I no longer know who I really am or what my dreams are? I don't think I've distanced myself on purpose. I'm not rebellious (like I used to be). I just think maybe I've been so disappointed in my own shortcomings, my wrong choices, and in the outcomes that have resulted, that I can't help but doubt my dreams.

More than that, *doubt* is perhaps not a strong enough word; I *fear* dreaming the wrong dream. I'm afraid that what I long for may not be your will for me or part of your plan. What if I've been dreaming the wrong dreams? You know what I'm talking about, I had a dream, and it shattered. Was I just fooling myself, thinking that my dream was your dream for me? Maybe I was just convincing myself that my desires were yours too, but I wasn't really asking.

God, your Word says that you give us the desires of our hearts (Psalm 37:4, NIV). Please, give me your desires. Put your will in my heart. I don't want to chase the wrong dreams anymore. I only want what you want. Give me the vision to see your will and pursue it. Give me a vision, lest I perish.

God, I want your dream.

Love,
Me

After writing this letter to my Father, the thought came to me, *I don't dream. I do.* I didn't know what to do with that idea at first, but the more I think about it, I wonder if God is telling me that he doesn't do the dreaming; that's our part. Rather, he puts the dream in our hearts; he gives us the vision. But then we have to pursue it because from where God sits, it's already a done deal. He's already empowered us with all we need to bring that vision to life. We just have to see it, believe it, and then through him, we can do it. "I can do all things through Christ who strengthens me" (Philippians 4:13).

The dream is already a reality to him. He's not sitting on the edge of his seat—his throne—just hoping and dreaming about his will being done. His will is done. He speaks, and it is. Didn't he create the whole world that way? But we have to proclaim his will, here on earth, and walk in it in order to live the life of our dreams. I believe that's why Jesus taught us how to pray, "Your kingdom come, your will be done, on earth as it is in heaven" (Matthew 6:10, NIV). It's already done in heaven, and we just need to bring it here. "Bring it on home!"

I love that! I love it because I can trust his Word and his will. That means I don't have to be scared of my own frailty. I love that when we pray the Lord's Prayer, we are calling what he has already spoken and established in heaven down to our lives here on earth. That's how we fulfil the purpose, the vision he gives us. That's how we live the life for which he gave us breath.

Dear Father,

It's me again. Any dream that I have ever had, or have, or will have, I lay at your feet. I only want it if you want it. Teach me your will for my life, give me the words to speak and confess, and I know you will accomplish all you have said.

As the rain and the snow
come down from heaven,
and do not return to it
without watering the earth
and making it bud and flourish,
so that it yields seed for the sower and bread
    for the eater,
so is my word that goes out from my mouth:
It will not return to me empty,
but will accomplish what I desire
and achieve the purpose for which I sent it.
(Isaiah 55:10–11, NIV)

Lord, teach me to echo the words of your sweet, submissive, Mary, "I am the servant of the Lord; let it be to me according to your word" (Luke 1:3–8, ESV). Teach me to live in this mind-set of submissiveness and continual yielding to your will. Even Jesus subjected his will to yours, "Yet not my will, but yours be done" (Luke 22:42, NIV). So, Father, if what I dream of is indeed part of your will and plan for my life, then thank you. If it's not, then remove the wrong desires from my heart and replace them with your own. I believe your Word and that you will stay with me and help me live out the dreams that *you* place in my heart.

Love,
Me

The Lord will work out his plans for my life—for your faithful love, O Lord, endures forever. Don't abandon me, for you made me. (Psalm 138:8, NLT)

A Flickering Candle

Have you ever felt like a flickering candle? You're holding on for dear life, but you know that if even the slightest wind passes by, that's it; you're out! I felt like that when I woke up this morning. I felt melted down by regret, remorse, and sin. Like those things were dripping all over me—like wax drips down a candle that's been burning for a while, burning out. I felt like I was nothing more than this tiny little wick, just barely flickering, trying to keep my light burning, but not knowing how much longer I could last.

And then the Lord quieted my heart with this reminder from his Word, "He will love you and not accuse you" (Zephaniah 3:18).

You see, there is a fine line between giving up and letting go, and I'm not good at either. As hard as I try to never give up, sometimes I have to learn to just let go. And I really need God's help with that because I hold onto my feelings of guilt and remorse to the point that I'm crippled by them. I know that's not what God wants for me. Once I repent (ask for forgiveness *and turn away from that sin*), he is faithful to forgive. He does not want me wallowing in shame. He forgets it, and he wants me to as well.

> I have made you, you are my servant;
> Israel, I will not forget you.
> I have swept away your offenses like a cloud,
> your sins, like the morning mist.
> Return to me, for I have redeemed you. (Isaiah 44:21–
> 22, NIV)

> For I will forgive their wickedness and will remem-
> ber their sins no more. (Hebrews 8:12, NIV)

I love how his promise to "forgive and forget" is in the future tense, and I don't think that is by accident. I believe it is because he knows that the devil will continue to blast us with accusations, and we will have to continue to rely on God's faithfulness all throughout our lives.

The devil can only keep piling it on, burying us beneath our guilt, until we stand up and say, "No! The Lord loves me and forgives me and will not accuse me." We have to fight the enemy with the Sword of the Spirit, which is the Word of God. Knowing that it is not God who is accusing and attacking us should be all we need to know to make us to pick up our sword and fight!

The devil is a liar, and he would like nothing more than to cripple and bury us beneath guilt and shame so that we cannot move forward and accomplish what God has created us to do, thus fulfilling our purpose in life. Why do we so often believe the liar rather than the Truth? If the Lord God is not accusing us, then who can?

> Who will bring any charge against those whom God has chosen? It is God who justifies. Who then is the one who condemns? No one. (Romans 8:33–34, NIV)

I believe what God says and he says, "I will not accuse them forever, nor will I always be angry, for then they would faint away because of me…the very people I have created" (Isaiah 57:16, NIV). God created us and loves us. He has compassion on us and does not want us to faint beneath the weight of our sin. He sent his only begotten Son to remove it from us. Why would he do that if he did not want us to be free from it?

He knew we couldn't remove it ourselves, and he knew we couldn't carry the guilt of it. That's why he sent Jesus—Jesus carried the weight of our sins and guilt to the cross. So now as long as we look to our Savior, Jesus Christ, and truly repent of and turn from our sins, then he removes them and remembers them no more. Why then should we?

> I, even I, am he who blots out your transgres-
> sions, for my own sake, and remembers your sins
> no more. (Isaiah 43:25, NIV)

I was going to quote a section of Psalm 103 here, but I think it's worth putting in the whole chapter. It's such a beautiful description of how God loves and forgives his children.

> Praise the Lord, my soul;
> all my inmost being, praise his holy name.
> Praise the Lord, my soul,
> and forget not all his benefits—
> who forgives all your sins
> and heals all your diseases,
> who redeems your life from the pit
> and crowns you with love and compassion,
> who satisfies your desires with good things
> so that your youth is renewed like the eagle's.
> The Lord works righteousness
> and justice for all the oppressed.
> He made known his ways to Moses,
> his deeds to the people of Israel:
> The Lord is compassionate and gracious,
> slow to anger, abounding in love.
> He will not always accuse,
> nor will he harbor his anger forever;
> he does not treat us as our sins deserve
> or repay us according to our iniquities.
> For as high as the heavens are above the earth,
> so great is his love for those who fear him;
> as far as the east is from the west,
> so far has he removed our transgressions from us.
> As a father has compassion on his children,

so the Lord has compassion on those who fear him;
for he knows how we are formed,
he remembers that we are dust.
The life of mortals is like grass,
they flourish like a flower of the field;
the wind blows over it and it is gone,
and its place remembers it no more.
But from everlasting to everlasting
the Lord's love is with those who fear him,
and his righteousness with their children's children—
with those who keep his covenant
and remember to obey his precepts.
The Lord has established his throne in heaven,
and his kingdom rules over all.
Praise the Lord, you his angels,
you mighty ones who do his bidding,
who obey his word.
Praise the Lord, all his heavenly hosts,
you his servants who do his will.
Praise the Lord, all his works
everywhere in his dominion.
Praise the Lord, O my soul. (Psalm 103, NIV)

Yes, "Praise the Lord, O my soul!"

Thank you, Father, that you discipline your children, but you do not stay angry with us forever. You do not repay us according to our iniquities or treat us as our sins deserve. Thank you for your compassion and mercy!

Thank you for being such a loving Father. Your discipline teaches me and instructs me; it inspires me to do better next time. Your discipline prunes me and helps me grow. You may get upset with me, but you do not hold a grudge. You do not harbor your anger once I repent. You don't beat me down or belittle me. You are slow to anger and abounding in love.

You don't snuff out my candle when I am weak, for your Word says, "A smoldering wick he will not snuff out."

Thank you, Father.

Love,
Me

He will not crush the weakest reed or put out a flickering candle. (Isaiah 42:3, NLT)

May I Have This Dance?

"Daddy, dance with me!" I can remember stepping onto my dad's giant shoes with my little ones and reaching up for his hands with mine. "Dance with me!" He would hold my hands and take giant steps, left and right, while I would hold on and try not to slip off his feet. It's a common picture, you'll see it on Father's Day cards all the time. (In fact, I think most of the Father's Day cards that I've bought my dad bear that image, it's precious to me.) I remember too how he would hum really loudly to make music as we "waltzed" around the house. Oh, how I loved dancing!

I was so excited when I finally got to take dance lessons! I was in kindergarten when I became a "ballerina." I say that with a laugh because I was definitely not prima ballerina material. But I didn't care, I had the shoes, the pink leotard, and tutu—I was content. You see, one of my earliest childhood memories is of lying in my bed (or it could have even been my crib, I don't know; it was in the first house I remember, and like I said, it's one of my very first memories) and staring up at the ballerina lamp that hung above me from the ceiling. When the light was on, the ballerinas would circle around in a graceful arabesque. I loved those ballerinas; I wanted to be one.

Years of ballet lessons later, I never did become a prima ballerina. I'm too tall, and I've never been that flexible or strong enough; to put it plainly, I was just never that good. Oh well, doesn't matter. I still love ballet, and even though I'll never be a "real ballerina," I'll settle for loving it anyway. After all, we don't have to be good at everything we love, right? I mean, I love music and singing too, and I have no talent in those areas either.

To some degree, the ability to dance is something you are born with. You either have it, or you don't. But to a much further degree, it's also something that can be learned. You may not have it at first, you may never really have it to the extent that you'd like it, but you can learn and get better over time, with hard work and practice. Like anything, you get out of it what you put into it.

Sometimes it's just a matter of being able to follow someone else's lead. For some of us, that's easier said than done. In the dance of life, I have spent too many years trying to do it my way. Believe me, the dance isn't pretty. I have learned that I need and want God for my partner. I want to follow his lead from now on. Only then will the dance be beautiful.

Dancing on my dad's feet, that was easy. It required no talent, only love. Dancing in a ballet class or in a recital was not as easy. And doing this dance we call life, well, that's just plain hard. It takes ability, it takes endurance, and sometimes, you just don't have it. You get knocked down, a lot, and you don't always make it through gracefully—not on your own anyway.

Butterflies and Ballerinas

Ballerinas don't always dance.
Butterflies don't always fly.
Sometimes it's just too much,
starin' up at that blue sky...

...so far away,
just let me stay,
leave me here to cry.

Just let me lie here,
I can't dance anymore.
It just got too hard,
gettin' cross that floor.

"Okay,"
he says,
"then just listen to the music,

I'm playing for you.
If all you can do is lie there,
then let me cover you with my song,
and I promise you,
my baby girl,
you won't be there very long…

For I'll wrap you in my love,
and rock you till you heal,
I'll hold you in my hands,
hold you till you kneel.

And kneelin's more than lying there,
and when you're ready to give me
every care—
then I'll take you by your hand,
and raise you to your feet,
and when you're ready to look up,
again,
our eyes will meet.

And when you're ready to move—
move on from all your pain,
I'll turn up
the music,
and you'll forget your shame.

And when you're ready to give yourself,
yet another chance,
my pretty ballerina,
it's then that you will dance.

And when you feel my song,
take your breath away,
you'll twirl around on tippy-toe—
your feet and heart will play.

And when you stretch your arms out,
relinquish that long-held sigh,
you'll leap and soar into my arms,
my little butterfly.

Because…
ballerinas always dance,
and butterflies always fly—
that's the way I made them,
and that's why."

God's Word promises us something wonderful; it says that he will turn our hard times and moments of sorrow into a beautiful dance. This is, perhaps, my most favorite scripture of all. "You have turned for me my mourning into dancing" (Psalm 30:11, NKJV). When I think about this, it gives me renewed hope and passion. I will dance and be happy again. All the falls, all the tears, and all the brokenness will one day be turned into joyful dancing. Then I will be like one of those little ballerinas that twirled around above my head. The ones I stared up at and dreamed to become. No more "unbecoming," but finally becoming who I was created to be—my Father's daughter.

This reminds me of a dream I had while in the process of writing this book. In my dream, I was in a ballet recital, and I was dancing (as usual) in the back. There were beautiful ballerinas in the rows in front of me, all gracefully, flawlessly dancing. But there I was, off in my own little corner in the back. It was more like I was dancing in the wings than on the stage. I felt really lost. Everybody else seemed to get it, knew the dance, and looked beautiful. But I was fumbling through, trying to catch on and catch up. Then I heard, "Dance in the light you've been given."

Following that direction, I tried to move out of the wing and farther onto the stage and into the light. It was so dark back there in the wing that I really had to focus on the light in order to step into it and dance.

As I think about that dream and what significance or meaning it may hold, I am realizing that the light is Jesus' presence—his forgiveness, his love, *him*. And the more we can focus on that light, the more we can step into it, and eventually "dance." We too can get it right and move throughout our lives with grace and beauty. "For in him we live and move and have our being" (Acts 17:28, NIV).

He said, "Dance in the light *you've been given*." I think that means with what you have already been given, dance. "Rejoice and be glad" (Matthew 5:12, NIV). In the life *you* have, not the life someone else has, or the life you think you should have, or thought you had, but in the life you have, right now—dance. Be thankful. Praise God for what you already have, for your life, at this moment. Like the Apostle Paul, learn "to be content whatever the circumstances" (Philippians 4:11, NIV).

It's so easy to stay in the corner, to surrender and surround ourselves in darkness, and ask, "What light?" We can insist that there is no light, or at least not enough to dance in. We could do that. And never dance. We can continue to complain and wallow in the wings, or we can focus on what little light we have been given and dance in it. It's the dance of thanksgiving that brings us, more and more, into the light of his presence. "Every good and perfect gift is from above, coming down from the Father of the heavenly lights, who does not change like shifting shadows" (James 1:17, NIV). Do you want to continue living your life in the shadows? Or can you muster up the strength, with his help, to step out from your sorrow and shame and step into the light of his presence?

You can have a thankful heart again even though your life's not perfect, even though you may still be sad or waiting for the answer to that prayer, that one you so desperately need. It's okay if you don't have it yet; thank God for it anyway. Even though you may not feel like it, you can still move into his light by praising him whatever your circumstances. Then and only then, will your heart dance and leap with joy. "The Lord is my strength and my shield; my heart trusts in him, and he helps me. My heart leaps for joy, and with my song I praise him" (Psalm 28:7, NIV).

Dance in the light you've been given.

Dear Father,

Help me to crawl out of the shadows and dance in the light you've given me. Help me to keep a thankful heart so that I can stay in your light. I don't want to ever allow myself, my mind, or my heart to be darkened no matter my circumstances. Keep me from slipping out of your presence and away from your light. I will praise you and worship you with a grateful heart for who you are, for all that you have already done, and by faith for all that you have in store. Praise your holy name, forever and ever! Amen.

Love,
Me

Let us come before him with thanksgiving and extol him with music and song. For the Lord is the great God, the great King above all gods. (Psalm 95:2–3, NIV)

Let them praise his name with dancing and make music to him with timbrel and harp. For the Lord takes delight in his people; he crowns the humble with victory. (Psalm 149:3–4, NIV)

Be thankful in all circumstances, for this is God's will for you who belong to Christ Jesus. (1 Thessalonians 5:18, NIV)

Again you will take up your timbrels and go out to dance with the joyful. (Jeremiah 31:4, NIV)

Nothing's Changed

I took my dad to the ER yesterday, and they admitted him for pneumonia. Today I'm just sitting here in his room, watching him, and keeping him company. It's finally quiet, and he's finally resting. He's so tired, but true to his job as Dad, he won't let me know how much he's suffering. He keeps telling me, "I'm fine, honey." He's one month shy of eighty-six, and his heart has been through a lot, including two heart attacks. They keep running all these tests and taking ultrasounds to determine the condition of his heart before doing a procedure to drain his lungs and get him breathing right again. I watch them and just keep thinking, *His physical heart might look weak to you, it might sound tired, but I can tell you the condition of his true heart. It's big. It's strong. It's good. It's the heart of a father.*

I got to thinking, *It's been years since I wrote my dad a letter.* I think it's time for another one, so here it goes. I won't be packing this one in his lunch box, but something tells me he'll treasure it just the same.

Dear Daddy,

I love you. How are you feeling? You look tired, I hope you can finally get some rest. I can't wait until we're out of this hospital room and back home. Then you can sleep without someone coming in every hour and eat some real food! I just want to be back home with you, sitting at your kitchen counter, playing cards, and solving all the world's problems, like we do.

I know you're feeling old, Daddy, but that's not how I see you. I still see you as a strong, hard-working man. I still see you as my protector. I still see your sparkly blue eyes that light up this whole room and everyone who walks in here. I still see your beautiful smile and feel its warmth. You're still my dad, and I still need you. You can't go anywhere yet, and even when you do, I know you'll still be with me.

I love you so much, Daddy. Thank you for loving me no matter what. I know there is nothing I could do that would ever change how much you love me. You're the only one who really gets me, and you still love me. You're the one person, on this earth, with whom I can just be myself—no role to fulfill, no expectations to reach, and no facade to put on. I can say anything, or nothing, and you understand.

Thank you for always making me laugh and knowing just how to comfort me. You can always bring a smile to my face and everyone else's (including every nurse who walks in here!). You always know how to make everyone feel so special. What a gift!

Thank you for being a picture of God's love, our Father in heaven. Thank you for being protective, understanding, forgiving, loving, and powerful.

You know that coffee mug I bought you, years ago? The one that says, "To My Daddy... the first man I ever loved." I remember how you laughed and thought that mug was so cute; you still have it. Thank you for being "My Daddy," and thank you for teaching me what love is.

Thank you for being constant. You're still "the best daddy in the whole wide world!"

Nothing's changed, despite how you may feel right now, I still feel like your little girl. Nothing's changed…nothing could. Yours is an unconditional, eternal kind of love. Thank you, Daddy. I love you sooooooooooo much!

Love,
Me

P.S. I'm glad you finally quit smoking five days ago. It may have taken me all these years to get you to quit, but you finally did.

XOXOXIXOXOXOXOXOXOXOXOXOXOX
OXOXOXOXOXOXOXOXOXOXOXOXOX
OXOXOOOXOXOXOXOXOXOXOXOXOX
OXOXOXOXOXOXOXOXOXOXOXOXOX
OXOXOXOXOXOXOXOXOXOXOXOXOX
OXOXOXOXOXOXOXOXOXOXOXOXOX
OXOXOXOXOXOXOXOXOXOXOXOXOX
OXOXOXOXOXOXOXOXOXOXOXOXOX
OXOXOXOXOXOXOXOXOXOXOXOXOX
OXOXOXOXOXOXOXOXOXOXOXOXOX
OXOXOXOXOXOXOXOXOXOXOXOXOX
OXOXOXOXOXOXOXOXOXOXOXOXOX
OXOXOXOXOXOXOXOXOXOXOXOXOX
OXOXOXOXOXOXOXOXOXOXOXOXOX
OXOXOXOXOXOXOXOXOXOXOXOXOX
OXOXOXOXOXOXOXOXOXOXOXOXOX
OXOXOXOXOXOXOXOXOXOXOXOXOX
OXOXOXOXOXOXOXOXOXOXOXOXOX
OXOXOXOXOXOXOXOXOXOXOXOXOX
OXOXOXOXOXOXOXOXOXOXOXOXOX
OXOXOXOXOXOXOXOXOXOXOXOXOX
OXOXOXOXOXOXOXOXOXOXOXOXOX

Believe

Thank God my dad made it out of the hospital and back home. I'm so grateful to still have him here with me. He's gone through so much, and despite his resistance and positive attitude, the years have taken their toll on him. He needs more help now, relies on me more, and I'm thankful I get to be here for him. Most of the time, it's just little things he needs, extra help around the house, fixing meals, etc. It's hard for me to watch him grow old because I know it's so frustrating for him to not be able to do what he once could. He doesn't like having his daughter take care of him because he still wants to take care of me. He doesn't realize how much he still does and how much I still need him. Like I said, I'm here doing little things, but for all the big things he has done for me, I am eternally grateful. It's not like I could ever begin to repay him for all he's done for me, but I'm glad that I get to show him my gratitude and love in this way.

Being there for my dad during this time in his life has been such a blessing. It's given me a chance not only to learn more about him while I still have him on this earth, but also to learn more about my Father in heaven through him. It's time well spent, time I'll never regret, time I'll never get back.

Ice cream has become my dad's new bad habit as age and doctors have deprived him of so many of his old favorites. So one night after bringing him a second bowl of ice cream, I sat on the floor next to his chair. He likes to eat his ice cream in his recliner, in front of the TV. We were just sitting there, and I was telling him about what was going on in my life. He already knew, but I was telling him, again.

I was telling him how I just really need God, right now like never before, to answer my prayers. You see, without going into detail here, I am desperate. And my dad knows how desperate I am.

He knows that I need God to answer this one—this one more than any other prayer I have ever prayed.

I know my dad could feel my pain. His eyes are not sharp enough for him to have seen the tears welling up in mine. His hearing, not good enough for him to have heard my voice shake and trail off in a hopeless effort to stop myself from crying. But he felt my pain. And he said, "God's gonna answer your prayers. Believe me, he won't forsake you."

The tears came, but so did the faith. Right then and there, I believed him. Just like that because I thought, *Well, if anyone knows, you do!* It may seem too simple to be true, but I cannot tell you how comforting it was to just believe him. But I really did, and I really do. I figured that if anyone knew how my Father up there saw things, it was my father down here. You see, he knows a little something about a father's love.

A Father's Love

It's a never leaving,
Always believing
The best in you,
Kind of love.

It's an "I'll search the world
And track you down,
I will not rest,
Till you're safe and sound,"
Kind of love.

It's a raging storm
When your heart's been torn,
And a shoulder to cry on,
When you're tired and worn,
Kind of love.

It's an "I think you're beautiful,"
When you know you're not.
It's an "I not only forgave you,
But I forgot,"
Kind of love.

It's a hand on your shoulder,
Just when you thought you were alone,
It's a "Hurry back, you know,
You'll always have a home,"
Kind of love.

It's an "I'd give my life,
Give it all for you,
No matter how you feel
Or what you do,"
Kind of love.

It's an "As long as I'm around,
You'll neither hunger nor thirst.
I love you more,
And I loved you first,"
Kind of love.

It's a strong arm,
And a protective hand.
It's the final word,
Line in the sand,
Kind of Love.

It's a mountain-moving,
Always-proving,
There's someone
Watching over you

From above.
It's always there,
It's all for you,
It's a Father's love.

When my dad told me, "He won't forsake you," I knew he knew what he was talking about. I believe him because he knows about that kind of love, the kind that will not let us down. My dad's love is the closest thing I have to that kind of love down here, so I believe him. He speaks from a place of authority.

I believe what my dad said, and I believe what my Father says. And believe me…there is power in believing! Just like you can believe the wrong things and really mess up your life, you can believe the right things and get it back!

If you've believed lies (which we all have), then you can believe the Truth. Jesus said, "According to your faith be it done to you" (Matthew 9:29, ESV). It's really a lot easier than you may think. Just believe what your Father says, that's it. End of story. "Close the book."

Afterthoughts and Challenge to Reader

Dear Reader,

Thank you for sharing in this journey with me, for taking the time to look into my life and more importantly into your own. My prayer is that you will grow closer and closer, every day, to your heavenly Father. He loves you so very much. He loves you more, and he loved you first. And he will love you forever and ever into all eternity. You did nothing to deserve it, but you got it anyway. He loves you no matter what.

If you want to step out of the shadows and into the light of his eternal love, then accept his forgiveness and praise him as the one true God. If you have never done so before, please pray this prayer with me right now, and you will be stepping into his light forever.

Dear Father,

I believe you, and I believe what you say. I believe you are God and that you sent your Son, Jesus, to pay the price for my sins and set me free. I ask you now to forgive me, Jesus, and come into my heart and change my life. I want you in my life, here and now, and I want to spend eternity with you in heaven. Thank you for loving me before I ever loved you. I trust you to take care of all the stuff I'm worried about, all the stuff I don't

understand—I just give it to you. And starting right now, I want to live my life in your presence. Thank you for never giving up on me, and now help me with this because you know better than anyone, I can't do it on my own. I accept you as my Lord and Savior, and yes, even my Father.
Amen.

It's that easy. You can and will be set free and have eternal salvation; all you have to do is ask. Your new life can start today, right now. Your Father loves you and wants to have an amazing relationship with you.

Here's my challenge to you. Pray to him just like you're talking to him. And when you can find the time or feel compelled to do so, write him letters. Remember these are just prayers on paper. They don't have to be flawless, no one is going to be correcting your grammar or spelling. No one else even has to read them. It's just about reaching the heart of God, and you do that with your heart (not with pretty words). So don't worry about what you write—just be honest. Write him letters (love letters, letters of petition, vent to him, whatever is in your heart). And then keep them, place them somewhere special that only you know about (maybe in a little box somewhere... maybe even a lunch box; you'll have your own lunch box letters). Then someday, you will look back on them, read through them, and smile to see how many times God has read every word, heard every cry, and answered.

Remember only God sees the big picture, and so you may not receive every answer you ask for, or at least not the way you thought you would, but God knows what he's doing. You can trust him; he's a good Father. Pour your heart out to him, both in word and on paper. He won't ignore your words, not one. He'll read every letter, every prayer, and store them in his heart (just like the best dad would).

Love,
Me

May the Lord bless and protect you; may the Lord's face radiate with joy because of you; may he be gracious to you, show you his favor, and give you his peace. (Numbers 6:24–26, TLB)

About the Author

Joey Tripoli grew up in Howell, Michigan. As a little girl, she started writing poetry, stories, and songs; and as she grew up, writing became one of her biggest passions and outlets. She graduated from Hope College in 1996 and then began her career as a teacher. Currently, she teaches seventh-grade English, and enjoys sharing her love of writing with her students. She also enjoys choreographing for children's theater programs in which she can combine her enthusiasm for teaching and her love of dance. *Lunch Box Letters* is a collection of the prayers and poems that once filled the pages of her journal, and now, her first book. Through this collection, she hopes to convey God's unconditional and unending love for us…*It's A Father's Love.*

CPSIA information can be obtained
at www.ICGtesting.com
Printed in the USA
LVHW100704200223
739869LV00001B/83

9 781645 595199